I0411449

FM 4-02.21

DIVISION AND BRIGADE SURGEONS' HANDBOOK (DIGITIZED)

TACTICS, TECHNIQUES, AND PROCEDURES

HEADQUARTERS, DEPARTMENT OF THE ARMY

FM 4-02.21

FIELD MANUAL
NO. 4-02.21

HEADQUARTERS
DEPARTMENT OF THE ARMY
WASHINGTON, DC, 15 November 2000

DIVISION AND BRIGADE SURGEONS™HANDBOOK (DIGITIZED) TACTICS, TECHNIQUES, AND PROCEDURES

TABLE OF CONTENTS

PREFACE

This publication provides information on the structure and operation of the division and brigade headquarters medical staff. It is directed toward the surgeons and staff members of the division surgeon's section (DSS) and brigade surgeon's section (BSS).

This field manual (FM) outlines the responsibilities of the division and brigade surgeons and their staffs for the heavy conservative divisions (digitized). It provides tactics, techniques, and procedures for directing, controlling, and managing combat health support (CHS) within the division. It describes the interface required of the DSS and BSS, other division elements, and the interface with supporting corps medical elements in accomplishing the CHS mission. It further defines each cell of the DSS and BSS. This manual is the foundation for the continued development and refinement of division CHS doctrinal fundamentals, tactics, techniques, and procedures for Army XXI. In that light, it serves as conceptual "mark on the wall" for thinking about experimenting with and employing new right-sized medical units/elements in the Army XXI light infantry, airborne and air assault divisions, separate brigades, and armored cavalry regiments.

This FM is not a stand-alone reference. It is a doctrine publication that speaks to the digitized division and brigade CHS and will require the user to be familiar with FMs 8-10, 8-10-1, 8-10-3, 8-10-4, 8-10-5, 8-10-6, 8-10-7, 8-10-9, 8-42, and 8-55. Users should also be familiar with the coordinating drafts of FMs 63-2-2, 63-20-1, 63-21-1, and 63-23-2.

This publication implements the following North Atlantic Treaty Organization (NATO) Standardization Agreements (STANAGs) and American, British, Canadian, and Australian (ABCA) Quadripartite Standardization Agreement (QSTAG):

Title	STANAG	QSTAG
Marking of Military Vehicles	2027	512
Orders for the Camouflage of the Red Cross and the Red Crescent on Land in Tactical Operations	2931	

When amendment, revision, or cancellation of this publication is proposed which will effect or violate the international agreements concerned, the preparing agency will take appropriate reconciliatory action through international standardization channels.

As the Army Medical Department (AMEDD) transitions to the 91W military occupational specialty (MOS), positions for 91B and 91C will be replaced by 91W when new unit modification table(s) of organization and equipment (MTOE) take effect.

Users of this publication are encouraged to submit comments and recommendations to improve the publication. Comments should include the page, paragraph, and line(s) of the text where the change is recommended. The proponent for this publication is the United States (US) Army Medical Department Center and School (AMEDDC&S). Comments and recommendations should be forwarded directly to **Commander, AMEDDC&S, ATTN: MCCS-FCD-L, 1400 East Grayson Street, Fort Sam Houston, Texas 78234-6175**, or by using the E-mail addresses on the Doctrine Literature website at *http://dcdd.amedd.army.mil/index1.htm* (click on Doctrine Literature).

Unless this publication states otherwise, masculine nouns and pronouns do not refer exclusively to men.

Use of trade or brand names in this publication is for illustrative purposes only and does not imply endorsement by the Department of Defense (DOD).

CHAPTER 1

DIVISION MEDICAL STAFF

Section I. DIVISION SURGEON

1-1.   Duties of the Division Surgeon

The division surgeon, a Medical Corps (MC) officer (Lieutenant Colonel [LTC], area of concentration [AOC] 60A00), is a division level special staff officer. He normally works under the staff supervision of the division chief of staff. The division surgeon is responsible for the technical control of all medical activities in the command. He oversees and coordinates CHS activities through the DSS. The division surgeon advises the division commander on all medical or medical-related issues. These issues include, but are not limited to—

- Health of the command.

- Preventive medicine (PVNTMED).

- Medical treatment provided to personnel in the division area of operations (AO).

- Status of wounded.

- Medical surveillance.

- Medical evacuation.

- Combat health logistics (CHL).

- Medical intelligence.

- Combat stress control (CSC).

- Dental services.

- Medical training.

- Civil-military operations.

1-2.   Responsibilities of the Division Surgeon

The division surgeon, assisted by the DSS, is responsible for—

- Advising on the health status of the command and of the occupied or friendly territory within the commander's area of responsibility.

- Briefing the division commander on CHS operations and/or his representative during all routine and emergency division briefings. This is normally accomplished using Combat Service Support Control System (CSSCS).

- Participating in the preparation of division operation plans (OPLANs) and contingency plans and identifying potential medical hazards associated with geographical locations and climatic conditions.

- Determining reporting frequencies (the times that reports are submitted) for digital reports using, Force XXI Battle Command Brigade and Below System (FBCB2) and CSSCS.

- Advising on the health effects of the environment.

- Advising on the health effects of nuclear, biological, and chemical (NBC) devices/weapons to include operational exposure guidance (OEG).

- Exercising technical supervision of subordinate brigade surgeons, physicians, and physician assistants (PAs).

- Providing consultation and mentoring to subordinate brigade surgeons, physicians, and physician assistants.

- Advising on the health effects of directed-energy devices/weapons.

- Determining requirements for the requisition, procurement, storage, maintenance, distribution management, and documentation of Class VIII supplies within the division.

- Providing the Assistant Chief of Staff (Logistics) (G4) a list of medical items that should be a part of the CSSCS commander's tracked items list (CTIL).

- Determining requirements for medical personnel and making recommendations concerning their assignments.

- Coordinating with medical unit commanders (to include leaders of medical platoons and sections) for continuous CHS.

- Submitting to higher headquarters those recommendations on professional medical problems that require research and development.

- Recommending use of captured medical supplies in support of enemy prisoners of war (EPW) and other recipients.

- Advising on medical intelligence requirements (including the examination and processing of captured medical supplies as directed by the corps surgeon).

- Providing recommendations on allocation and redistribution of AMEDD personnel, CHL, and CHS during the reconstitution process.

- Advising commanders about the PVNTMED aspects of reconstitution and availability and use of CSC teams.

- Forwarding the Command Health Report (RCS MED-3 [R7]) according to Chapter 3, Army Regulation (AR) 40-5.

- Advising commanders on the effects of accumulated fatigue, radiation exposure, possible delayed effects from exposure to chemical or biological agents, and use of countermeasures and pre-treatments.

- Advising commanders on disposition of personnel exposed to lethal, but not immediately life-threatening, doses of radiation or chemical and biological agents.

- Preparing the division CHS annex to all division plans. For CHS planning factors, see FM 8-55.

- Ensuring that clear and accurate patient records are maintained of all clinical encounters for supported deployed personnel through the use of a Department of the Army (DA) Form 8007-R or through the use of digital patient records as they become available. See AR 40-66 and FM 8-10-1 for management of individual health records in the field. Also, digital patient records at the division and brigade level will be available through the fielding of Medical Communications for Combat Casualty Care (MC4) and the Theater Medical Information Program (TMIP).

NOTE

The purpose of a medical record is to provide a complete medical and dental history for patient care, medicolegal support (for example, reimbursement and tort claims), research, and education. A medical record also provides a means of communication where necessary to fulfill other Army functions (such as, identification of remains). Therefore, each time a patient encounter occurs, an entry will be made on the medical record. It is the responsibility of the division and brigade surgeons to ensure that written or digital entries made in patient records in the field are transcribed or downloaded to the patients' permanent medical or dental records as soon as possible.

Section II. DIVISION SURGEON'S SECTION

1-3.   Missions and Capabilities of the Division Surgeon's Section

a.   The DSS's mission is to plan, coordinate, and synchronize the division's CHS under the supervision of the division surgeon.

b.   The DSS is also responsible for coordinating relationships of organic medical units and medical units/elements under operational control (OPCON) or attached to the division for general support (GS) or direct support (DS).

1-4.   Organization

Figure 1-1 shows the typical organization and staffing of the DSS. The DSS is normally located with the division main and consists of a medical plan and operations cell, a CHL cell, a patient disposition and reports cell, and a PVNTMED cell.

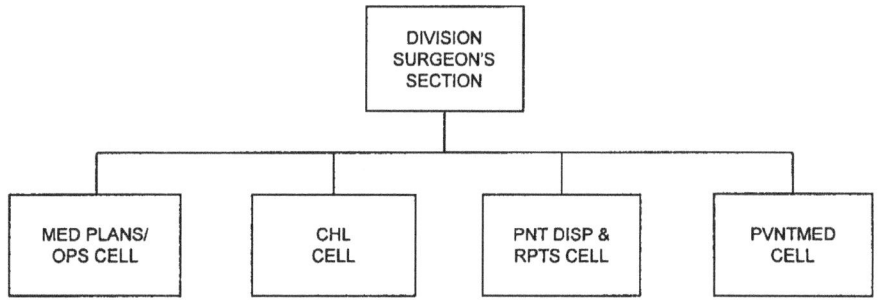

Figure 1-1. Division surgeon's section.

a.   *Medical Plans and Operations Cell.* The medical plans and operations cell is responsible for—

•   Developing and coordinating patient evacuation support plans among the division and corps medical evacuation elements.

•   Coordinating corps-level CHS for the division with the corps medical command (MEDCOM)/brigade.

•   Submitting Army airspace command and control (A2C2) requirements for aeromedical evacuation elements to the division Assistant Chief of Staff (Operations and Plans) (G3) (Air).

- Ensuring A2C2 information is provided to supporting corps air ambulance assets. The A2C2 information is normally provided by the G3 (Air) at division and by the brigade Operations and Training Officer (US Army) (S3) (Air) in the maneuver brigades.

- Coordinating for aviation weather information from US Air Force (USAF) weather (WX) detachment in the aviation brigade.

- Obtaining updated road clearance information from the division movement control office (MCO). All road clearance information is passed to ground ambulance assets. This information should include—

  - The NBC threat.

  - Priorities for use of evacuation routes.

  - Information reported by medical evacuation assets.

  - Road and weather conditions.

  - Security.

- Monitoring medical troop strength to determine task organization for mission accomplishment.

- Forwarding all medical information of potential intelligence value to the division Assistant Chief of Staff (Intelligence) (G2) and G3 staffs.

- Obtaining updated medical threat and intelligence information through the G2 and G3 staff for evaluation and applicability.

- Managing the disposition of captured medical materiels according to tactical standing operating procedures (TSOPs).

- Coordinating corps CSC support to forward areas as required.

- Monitoring optometry services.

The medical plans and operations cell is typically staffed with a—

- Chief medical planner.

- Plans and operations officer, medical evacuation.

- Plans and operations officer.

- Chief operations sergeant.

- Senior medical noncommissioned officer (NCO).

- Medical intelligence NCO.

- Medical operations sergeant.

(1) *Chief Medical Planner.* The chief medical planner (LTC, AOC 70H67) assists the division surgeon with developing and maintaining the medical troop basis. He recommends task organization for mission accomplishment. He is the chief of the medical plans and operations cell. He is the primary architect of the division CHS plan, based on the division commander's intent and guidance from the division surgeon. He monitors brigade and division operations to ensure adequacy of CHS for the supported force.

(2) *Plans and Operations Officer, Medical Evacuation.* The plans and operations officer for medical evacuation (Captain, AOC 67JOO) coordinates patient evacuation to corps-level medical facilities by Army assets. This officer develops and coordinates medical evacuation plans with the supporting corps-level and joint medical elements. He coordinates with division A2C2 elements to ensure that the supporting corps aeromedical evacuation units receive up-to-date overlays and A2C2 information. He coordinates for aviation weather information from the USAF WX detachment in the aviation brigade.

(3) *Plans and Operations Officer.* The plans and operations officer (Major, AOC 70H67) assists the medical planner with developing and coordinating the division CHS plan. He monitors and tracks CHS operations and updates the chief medical planner and division surgeon as necessary. He coordinates with division command and control (C2) elements to ensure task organization for mission accomplishment. This officer deploys with the division forward tactical operations center (TOC).

(4) *Chief Operations Sergeant.* The chief operations sergeant (E-9, MOS 91B50) assists the medical planner in accomplishing his operational duties. He coordinates and supervises the administration functions within the DSS.

(5) *Senior Medical Noncommissioned Officer.* The senior medical NCO (E-8, MOS 91B50) assists the medical planner. He assists the chief operations sergeant with supervising the activities of subordinate enlisted personnel assigned to this branch.

(6) *Medical Intelligence Noncommissioned Officer.* The medical intelligence NCO (E-7, MOS 91B40) reviews medical information of potential intelligence value. He coordinates with the G2 and G3 to receive and pass medical information of potential intelligence value and intelligence of a medical nature. He works in conjunction with the G2 staff in determining likely threat movement and expected actions that will affect CHS requirements. He assists in coordinating the disposition of captured medical materiel with the medical logistics (MEDLOG) battalion. This NCO prepares and monitors the division medical intelligence program.

(7) *Medical Operations Sergeant, Medical Evacuation.* The medical operations sergeant (E-6, MOS 91B30) assists the plans and operations officer, medical evacuation in accomplishing his duties.

b. *Combat Health Logistics Cell.* The CHL cell is responsible for planning, coordinating, and prioritizing CHL and medical equipment maintenance programs for the division. The specific responsibilities of the CHL cell include the following:

- Providing the division CHL input to the CHS plan through the plans and operations cell.

- Coordinating medical maintenance training.

- Establishing maintenance priorities for repair and exchange of medical equipment with the MEDLOG company (ensuring that critical items are included on the division CSSCS/FBCB2 CTIL).

- Ensuring that a viable preventive maintenance program is established and monitored.

- Coordinating the evacuation and replacement of medical equipment with the MEDLOG company.

- Verifying emergency supply requests for submission to the supporting MEDLOG company and taking the necessary action to expedite shipment.

- Analyzing Class VIII resupply operations, identifying trends in performance, and providing technical advice, as necessary.

- Establishing and managing, in coordination with the division support command (DISCOM) medical materiel management branch (MMMB), the medical critical items list.

- Interfacing with the DISCOM MMMB to ensure that the necessary coordination with the division supply and transportation system occurs.

- Establishing transportation procedures, based on the tactical situation, with the MEDLOG company and DISCOM MMMB.

- Providing technical staff assistance for the DISCOM MMMB and division medical unit/ elements, as required, to ensure divisionwide support for CHL and blood management.

- Monitoring the CHL picture and reporting its status using CSSCS.

- Establishing coordination procedures for the disposition of captured medical materiel.

- Prioritizing Class VIII supply requests and distribution, as required.

The CHL cell is staffed with a health service materiel officer (HSMO). The HSMO (Major, AOC 70K67) works closely with the DISCOM MMMB and MEDLOG company. The HSMO coordinates and oversees the CHL support for the division.

c. *Patient Disposition and Reports Cell.* The patient disposition and reports cell is responsible for coordinating patient disposition throughout the division. The branch obtains and coordinates disposition of patients with the medical plans and operations cell and the corps medical regulating office(r) (MRO). It prepares and forwards appropriate medical statistical reports as required. The patient disposition and reports cell is staffed with a patient administration NCO and two patient administration specialists.

(1) *Patient Administration Noncommissioned Officer.* The patient administration NCO (E-5, MOS 71G20) assists the operations officer, medical evacuation in the coordination of patient disposition in the division. This NCO prepares the required patient statistical reports and coordinates their timely submission to higher headquarters. He also supervises the patient administration specialists.

(2) *Patient Administration Specialists.* The two patient administration specialists (E-4, MOS 71G10) assist the patient administration NCO in preparing patient statistical reports and in performing other patient administration functions. They also operate the Tactical Army CSS Computer System (TACCS).

d. *Preventive Medicine Cell.* The division PVNTMED cell is responsible for—

- Supervising the command PVNTMED program; see AR 40-5 and FM 4-02.17 (8-10-17).

- Ensuring PVNTMED measures are implemented that protect division personnel against food-, water-, and vectorborne diseases, as well as environmental injuries (for example, heat and cold injuries).

- Monitor disease trends within the division.

The PVNTMED missions are accomplished according to the division CHS plan and coordinated by the PVNTMED officer through the medical plans and operations cell with the division support medical company and forward support medical companies (FSMCs). Division PVNTMED personnel provide advice and consultation in the areas of environmental sanitation, epidemiology, and entomology, as well as limited sanitary engineering services and pest management. Additional information pertaining to the PVNTMED personnel and their specific functions is discussed in FMs 8-10, 8-10-1, 8-10-3 and 4-02.17 (8-10-17). The PVNTMED cell is staffed with a PVNTMED officer. The PVNTMED officer (Major, AOC 60C00) is responsible for the implementation of the command PVNTMED program. The PVNTMED officer determines the status of and conditions influencing the health of units located in the division AO. He formulates and recommends measures for health improvements. Based on command, corps, and theater Army (TA) guidance, he plans, directs, and prioritizes PVNTMED activities within the division. The PVNTMED officer serves as the principal advisor on medical threats encountered by division units. He recommends PVNTMED measures to minimize these threats within the division AO. He is also involved in PVNTMED activities that must begin prior to deployment to minimize disease and nonbattle injury (DNBI). Actions taken prior to deployment must include—

- Performing medical threat analysis.

- Ensuring command awareness of potential medical threats and that appropriate PVNTMED measures are being implemented.

- Monitoring immunization and chemoprophylaxis status of division personnel.

- Monitoring the status of individual and small unit PVNTMED measures.

- Monitoring PVNTMED measures against heat and cold injuries and food-, water-, and vectorborne diseases.

- Preparing PVNTMED estimates.

Planning considerations must include the following issues:

- Water.

- Environmental conditions.

- Vectors.

- Food.

- Waste/sanitation.

- Nuclear, biological, and chemical.

1-5. Functions

The staff of the DSS assists the division surgeon in planning and conducting division CHS operations. Specific functions of the DSS include—

- Planning and ensuring that Echelons I and II CHS for the division is provided in a timely and efficient manner.

- Developing and maintaining the medical troop basis, revising as required, to ensure task organization for mission accomplishment.

- Planning and coordinating CHS operations for division and attached/OPCON corps medical assets. This includes reinforcement and reconstitution.

- Preparing and presenting, as directed by the division surgeon, routine CHS portion of the division briefings.

- Coordinating with the G3 for prioritizing the reallocation of organic and corps medical augmentation assets as required by the tactical situation.

- Overseeing division TSOPs, plans, policies, and procedures for CHS as prescribed by the division surgeon.

- Overseeing individual and collective medical training and providing information to the division surgeon and division commander.

- Coordinating and prioritizing CHL and blood management requirements for the division.

- Coordinating with the Assistant Chief of Staff (Personnel) (G1) for tracking critical AOC and MOSs.

- Monitoring disease trends within the division.

- Collecting and disseminating medical threat information and coordinating combat health intelligence requirements with the division G2 according to FM 8-10-8.

- Facilitating functional integration between CHS and military intelligence staff elements within the division. This is done in support of the intelligence preparation of the battlefield.

- Coordinating and redirecting patient evacuation within the division.

- Coordinating patient evacuation from division-level medical treatment facilities (MTFs) to corps-level MTFs.

- Coordinating with the G3, G4, and division chemical officer for nonmedical assets for assisting with mass casualties and patient decontamination operations.

- Coordinating with the G3 for additional corps evacuation assets, as required.

- Coordinating the medical evacuation of all EPW casualties.

- Coordinating and managing the disposition of captured medical materiel.

- Coordinating, planning, and prioritizing PVNTMED missions.

- Coordinating corps dental support when the tactical situation permits.

- Coordinating with the supporting veterinary element pertaining to subsistence and animal disease surveillance.

- Developing and publishing the medical reporting schedule for FBCB2 (medical situation report [MEDSITREP]), CSSCS (medical unit status reporting), evacuation requests, and other reports as necessary.

Section III. STAFF AND COMMAND INTERFACE

1-6. Interface with the Division Staff

   a. The G1 provides and coordinates personnel support for the division. The G1's functions are listed in FM 101-5.

   (1) The G1's responsibilities include—

   (a) Tracking critical medical AOCs and MOS.

   (b) Reporting casualties.

   (c) Conducting replacement operations.

   (d) Making casualty projections for the division.

   (e) Monitoring patient evacuation and mortality.

   (2) Reports submitted from the DSS to the G1 should be identified in the division TSOP. These reports can vary depending on the needs of the command and are submitted using CSSCS.

   (3) The DSS and the G1 staff must work together and coordinate their staff and operational activities to ensure mission accomplishment.

   b. The G2 and G3 staffs are primarily involved with plans, operations, intelligence, and security. The functions of the G2 and G3 are listed in FM 101-5.

   c. The G4 functions are listed in FM 101-5. The G4 is primarily concerned with the logistical status of the division. The G4 has the responsibility for planning and supervising the supply, service, maintenance, and transportation activities to support the command.

   d. The Assistant Chief of Staff (Civil Affairs) (G5) functions are listed in FM 101-5. These functions include those actions that embrace the relationship between the command and host nation (HN), civil authorities and the local nationals in the AO.

   e. The DSS works with other division staff elements to inform, coordinate, and achieve synchronization of CHS activities for division operations. Examples of the coordination that must take place between the DSS and other division staff elements are shown in Table 1-1. The division surgeon, the DSS chief medical planner, and other DSS staff members must be informed of division staff activities and be involved with the decision-making process. Areas of mutual interest are shown in Table 1-2.

Table 1-1. Coordination Between Division Surgeon's Section and Division Staff

SUBJECT AREA	DIVISION STAFF ELEMENT	DSS
PLANNING	G2/G3/G4	MED PLANS/OPS CELL CHL CELL
RELOCATING CHS ELEMENTS	G2/G3/G4	MED PLANS/OPS CELL
PREVENTIVE MEDICINE	G1/G2/G3/G4/G5 DIV FOOD ADVISOR	MED PLANS/OPS CELL PVNTMED CELL
MEDICAL SUPPORT REQUEST	G3/G5	MED PLANS/OPS CELL CHL CELL
MEDICAL INFORMATION OF POTENTIAL INTELLIGENCE VALUE	G2	MED PLANS/OPS CELL PVNTMED CELL
CORPS SUPPORT MEDICAL ELEMENTS MEDICAL ELEMENTS	G1/G3/G4	MED PLANS/OPS CELL CHL CELL
CIVIL AFFAIRS ACTIVITIES	G5/G3/G2	MED PLANS/OPS CELL PVNTMED CELL
CLASS VIII RESUPPLY	G4/G3 DIV MCO/DTO	CHL CELL MED PLANS/OPS CELL
NUCLEAR, BIOLOGICAL, CHEMICAL DEFENSE SMOKE/OBSCURATION	G2/G3	MED PLANS/OPS CELL PVNTMED CELL
ENEMY PRISONER OF WAR OPERATIONS	G2/G3	MED PLANS/OPS CELL
MAINTENANCE	G4	MED PLANS/OPS CELL CHL CELL
CASUALTY ESTIMATES AND REPORTING	G1	MED PLANS/OPS CELL PNT DISP & RPT CELL
A2C2	G3 (AIR)	MED PLANS/OPS CELL
HEALTH CARE POLICY	G1/G3	DIV SURGEON MED PLANS/OPS CELL

Table 1-2. Areas of Mutual Interest for Division Surgeon's Section and Division Staff

SUBJECT	DIVISION STAFF SECTION
MEDICAL INFORMATION OF A POTENTIAL INTELLIGENCE VALUE OR INTELLIGENCE OF A MEDICAL NATURE	G2
COMBAT HEALTH SUPPORT	G1/G3
CONTINGENCY OPERATIONS	G3
REPLACEMENT AND RECONSTITUTION OPERATIONS	G1/G3/G4
PREVENTIVE MEDICINE	G1/G2/G3/G4/G5
CIVIL AFFAIRS/HOST-NATION SUPPORT	G5/G2/G3/G4
INTERNMENT/RESETTLEMENT (I/R) OPERATIONS	G1/G2/G3
MASS CASUALTY PLAN	G1/G2/G3/G4
NUCLEAR, BIOLOGICAL, CHEMICAL DEFENSE	G1/G2/G3/G4

1-7. Interface with the Major Commands of the Division

a. Maneuver Brigades. Interface with each of the maneuver brigades is accomplished through the BSS and through the DISCOM support operations section, DISCOM medical operations branch, and the health service support officers (HSSOs) of the division support battalion (DSB) and forward support battalions (FSBs) and other staff elements as appropriate. This interface will focus on CHL and CHS requirements for the brigades. It also includes coordination for A2C2 information for air evacuation assets supporting maneuver elements.

b. Aviation Brigade. Interactions between the aviation brigade and the DSS should include—

(1) Coordination for area medical support.

(2) Coordination for evacuation of patients using helicopters with heavy lift capabilities.

(3) Coordination for air delivery of Class VIII emergency resupply.

(4) Coordination for appropriate aviation plans and overlays supporting division operations.

(5) Coordination for aviation logistics support (aviation fuel maintenance and spare parts) to support air ambulances, when required.

(6) Coordination for aviation weather information from the USAF WX detachment in the aviation brigade.

(7) Coordination through the division aviation support battalion (DASB) CHS requirements for the aviation brigade and the division cavalry squadron. For further discussion, see FM 63-23-2.

c. Division Support Command. Interface with the DISCOM will include most of its staff elements.

(1) The Adjutant (US Army) (S1) provides and coordinates personnel support for the command. The DISCOM S1's responsibilities are listed in FM 63-2-2.

(a) Some of the S1's responsibilities include—

- Tracking critical AOCs and MOS by skill indicators.

- Reporting casualties.

- Conducting replacement operations.

- Making casualty projections for the DISCOM.

- Monitoring patient evacuation and mortality.

(b) Reports submitted from the medical operations cell, DISCOM to the S1 should be identified in the DISCOM TSOP. These reports can vary depending on the needs of the command.

(c) The DSS and DISCOM medical operation branches work together and coordinate their staff and operational activities to ensure mission accomplishment.

(2) The Intelligence Officer (US Army)(S2)/S3 section is primarily involved with plans, operations, intelligence, and security. The elements of the S2/S3 and its numerous responsibilities are listed in FM 63-2-2.

(a) Elements of the DSS, DISCOM medical operations cell and elements of the S2/S3 work together to synchronize CHS activities to division operations. The DSS will use its CSSCS to receive and transmit information and prepare briefings, overlays and plans with the DISCOM staff. Examples of the coordination that must take place between elements of the DSS, DISCOM medical operations cell and elements of the DISCOM S2/S3 section are shown in Table 1-3.

(b) The DISCOM support operations officer, DISCOM S2/S3 and the DSS chief medical planner must be informed of staff activities and be involved with the decision-making process.

(3) The DISCOM Supply Officer (US Army) (S4) is responsible for all logistics matters pertaining to DISCOM units. The DISCOM S4's responsibilities are listed in FM 63-2-2.

(a) The DSS coordinates with the DISCOM S4 for logistical requirements, other than medical, that impact on CHS operations.

(b) The DSS must coordinate with the S4 for critical supply items list (nonmedical) requirements.

Table 1-3. Coordination Between Division Surgeon's Section and Division Support Command

SUBJECT AREA	DISCOM	DSS
PLANNING	S2/S3 PLANS-INTEL BR DMC MED OPS BR DMC OPS SEC GSO MMMB	MED INTEL NCO MED PLANS/OPS CELL MED PLANS/OPS CELL HSMO
RELOCATING CHS ELEMENTS	DMC OPS SEC DMC MED OPS BR	MED PLANS/OPS CELL
PREVENTIVE MEDICINE	DMC OPS SEC S4 DIV FOOD ADVISOR S2/23 PLANS-INTEL BR MED INTEL NCO PVNTMED CELL MED PLANS/OPS CELL	MED PLANS/OPS CELL PVNTMED CELL PVNTMED CELL
MEDICAL SUPPORT REQUEST	S2/S3 OFC S2/S3 PLANS-INTEL BR GSO MMMB DMC OPS SEC	MED PLANS/OPS CELL MED INTEL NCO CHL CELL MED PLANS/OPS CELL

MEDICAL INFORMATION OF POTENTIAL
   INTELLIGENCE VALUE OR
   INTELLIGENCE A MEDICAL NATURE
	S2/S3 PLANS-INTEL BR
	DMC MED OPS BR
		MED INTEL NCO
		MED PLANS/OPS CELL
		PVNTMED CELL

CORPS SUPPORT	DMC OPS SEC DMC MED OPS BR	MED PLANS/OPS CELL
MEDICAL ELEMENTS CIVIL AFFAIRS ACTIVITIES	S2/S3 PLANS-INTEL BR	MED PLANS/OPS CELL PVNTMED CELL
CLASS VII RESUPPLY	GSO MMMB DMC MED OPS BR DMC OPS SEC MCO	CHL CELL MED PLANS/OPS CELL CHL CELL CHL CELL
NUCLEAR, BIOLOGICAL, CHEMICAL DEFENSE SMOKE/OBSCURATION ENEMY PRISONER OF WAR OPERATIONS MAINTENANCE	S2/S3 PLANS-INTEL BR S2/S3 PLANS-INTEL BR S2/S3 PLANS-INTEL BR SPT OPS SEC MAINT MGT OFC GSO MMMB	PVNTMED CELL MED PLANS/OPS CELL MED PLANS/OPS CELL MED PLANS/OPS CELL MED PLANS/OPS CELL CHL/PVNTMED CELL
NUTRITION INITIATIVES AND MENU APPROVAL	S4 DIV FOOD ADVISOR	DIV SURGEON
USE OF DIGITAL SYSTEMS	S6	MED OPS OFFICER

1-8.   Interface with the Corps Medical Units

Interface with corps medical units is accomplished through the corps MEDCOM/brigade. Direct interface can occur with those medical units providing support to the division and will be coordinated by the DSS and the corps staff. The MEDCOM/brigade will provide subordinate units to support the division by establishing a command relationship of OPCON or attachment. The MEDCOM/brigade could also choose to maintain only a support relationship of DS or GS to support the division. The DSS interfaces with corps medical units according to the MEDCOM/brigade TSOP. The DSS and other division staff elements must be prepared to integrate corps-level medical units/elements into the medical, as well as the logistical, support structure. The MEDCOM/brigade will normally deploy a liaison officer to the division to coordinate and synchronize corps CHS. Information concerning the organization, functions, and responsibilities of the corps MEDCOM/brigade is found in FM 8-10.

    a.   Corps Medical Command and Medical Brigade. The corps MEDCOM and medical brigade provide C2, including—

- Staff planning.

- Supervision of operations.

- Administration of the assigned and attached units.

    (1)   The following areas are subjects of mutual concern for division and corps medical staff elements:

- Medical regulating.

- Division CHS requirements.

- Ground and air ambulance support.

- Class VIII resupply, blood management, and medical maintenance.

- Status of corps medical elements attached, or OPCON, to the division.

- Disease surveillance.

- Medical threat and intelligence estimates.

- Captured medical supplies and equipment.

- Reinforcement and reconstitution of CHS elements.

- Civil affairs and HN support.

- Communications.

- Locations of medical elements in support of the division.

- Preventive medicine, mental health, dental, or veterinary assistance.

(2) Logistical support requirements for corps medical elements operating in the division are identified and coordinated with the corps support battalion. When corps medical elements deploy to the division, logistical support is normally provided by the corps support battalion. Coordination could be required for—

- Class I—Subsistence items and gratuitous issue health and welfare items.

- Class II—Items of equipment other than principal items which are prescribed in authorization and allowance tables (individual equipment, clothing items, tents, tool sets, and administrative and housekeeping supplies).

- Class III—Petroleum, oils, and lubricants (POL) (petroleum fuels, hydraulic and insulating oils, chemical products, antifreeze compounds, compressed gases, and coal).

- Class IV—Construction and barrier materials, lumber, sandbags, and barbed wire.

- Class V—Ammunition.

- Class VI—Personal demand items such as health and hygiene products (soap and toothpaste), writing material, snack food, beverages, batteries, and cameras (nonmilitary sales items).

- Class VII—Major end items—(final combination of items which are ready [assembled] for intended use).

- Class VIII and Blood—Medical materiel, including repair parts peculiar to medical equipment, and blood products

- Class IX—Repair parts.

- Field services (billeting, showers, and services).

- Personnel replacements (corps supported).

b. Medical Logistics Battalion. The MEDLOG battalion is organic to the corps medical brigade. The MEDLOG battalion provides C2 for assigned MEDLOG companies and the blood support detachment. The MEDLOG battalion is responsible for receiving, storing, and distributing medical materiel; single and multivision optical fabrication and repair; medical maintenance; blood and blood product collection, manufacturing, and distribution; medical gas production and distribution; and building of medical assemblages/push packages. The MEDLOG battalion will employ standard state-of-the-art MEDLOG information management and communications systems to include satellite links. Interface between the DSS and the MEDLOG battalion, MEDLOG company, or blood support detachment could be required for—

- Emergency Class VIII resupply.

- Repair of medical equipment.

- Blood management.

- Optical fabrication requirements.

- Management of captured medical materiel.

- Storage and decontamination techniques to minimize NBC contamination of Class VIII supplies.

(1) *Medical logistics company.* The MEDLOG company provides Class VIII supplies, DS/GS medical maintenance, and optical support. The MEDLOG company will use line item requisitioning to support customers and will have the capabilities of building and maintaining preconfigured push packages in support of forward deployed medical units.

(2) *Blood support detachment.* The MEDLOG battalion's blood support detachment serves as the Army's blood supply unit (BSU). Blood and blood products will be stored and distributed under rigid specifications and managed by standard automated systems. Air movement will be the mode of choice for transporting blood and blood products. Army blood support in the AO will be the responsibility of the supporting MEDLOG battalion. The MEDLOG battalion's blood support detachment will collect and manufacture, receive, store, and distribute blood and blood products on an area basis.

c. Medical Evacuation Battalion. The headquarters and headquarters detachment, medical evacuation battalion serves as the central manager of ground and air evacuation assets in the corps. Its mission is to provide C2 of ground and air medical evacuation units within its AO. Information pertaining to the organization, functions, and capabilities of this unit is discussed in FM 8-10-6. The DSS interfaces with the medical evacuation battalion or subordinate units concerning—

- Air and ground movement liaison within the division AO.

- Reinforcement of division CHS assets.

- Mass casualty evacuation plans.

- Evacuation of patients from division to supporting corps hospitals.

- Emergency movement of medical personnel, supplies, and blood.

- Ambulance shuttle operations, to include ambulance exchange points (AXPs) and patient collection points.

- The status of medical evacuation battalion elements operating in the division.

- Management and decontamination of ground/air evacuation assets.

- Support requirements for forward deployed medical evacuation battalion assets.

- Location of medical evacuation battalion assets.

- Location of division medical elements.

- The tactical situation and threat updates.

- Delivery of blood and blood products.

- Reinforcement of covering force and deep operations evacuation assets.

- Road and movement clearances.

- Maintenance support, to include aviation intermediate maintenance (AVIM).

- Emergency resupply of medical and nonmedical items (if required).

- Communications requirements and signal operation instructions (SOI).

- Updated tactical maps and evacuation overlays.

- Terrain considerations and barrier plans for ambulances.

- Evacuation destinations (MRO functions).

- Division and brigade A2C2 requirements.

- Combat search and rescue missions.

(1)   Within the division area, the air ambulance company provides aeromedical evacuation on a DS basis. This company is normally attached for support (less OPCON) to the division aviation brigade. Air ambulances will operate from the division support area (DSA) and brigade support areas (BSAs) providing 24-hour immediate response medical evacuation capability.

(2)   Successful aeromedical evacuation support to the division requires current and accurate operational information. This information includes A2C2, current intelligence, friendly situation, air traffic service procedures, weather, combat service support (CSS), and aviation safety and standardization data. To enhance the safety and effectiveness of aeromedical operations, operations information should flow between air ambulance units and the GS aviation battalion or assault helicopter battalion of the respective aviation brigade.

(3) Information is exchanged by various methods including on-site coordination or communications systems. The air ambulance company can obtain information through various sources such as the DSS and BSSs of the maneuver brigade TOCs. However, during the planning and execution phases of operations, the medical evacuation battalion and the aviation unit to which the air ambulance company is attached are the primary sources for providing this information. The DSS also provides A2C2 planning information to the air ambulance company. This information includes, but is not limited to, the following:

- Location of medical units.

- Locations of forward arming and refueling points.

- Liaison requirements with supported units.

- Evacuation corridors recommendation.

The air ambulance company, in turn, continually provides the medical evacuation battalion, aviation brigade, and DSS with updated information about its current and planned operations. The company also provides pertinent combat information obtained during missions. This information includes threat disposition, downed aircraft, weather, and other factors obtained by air ambulance crews during the performance of their duty. All medical evacuation crews communicate directly with the division air traffic service and execute A2C2 while operating behind brigade boundaries.

(4) When air ambulances operate in the DSA, they execute the A2C2 plan and communicate directly with the division air traffic service. Emergency requests for aeromedical evacuation is relayed as necessary from the DSS through the DSMC to the air ambulance elements position at their location for the mission.

(5) Air ambulances deployed forward into the BSA normally collocate with the FSB or aviation task force. When deployed forward to the BSA, the air ambulance team's evacuation missions are coordinated by the FSMC commander. The FSMC assisted by the support operations section provides real-time tactical information to the air ambulance crew about evacuation missions from the maneuver battalion/company to the brigade rear area. When air ambulances operate forward of the BSA, they will execute the A2C2 plan through the maneuver brigade S3. The FSB support operations section provides planning and coordination between aeromedical evacuation and the supported maneuver brigade. The brigade S3 provides the A2C2 plan which includes the air corridors, air control points, and communications checkpoints. The brigade S3 will provide updates as required. Air ambulances deployed to the BSA will normally provide medical evacuation from forward areas (battalion aid station [BAS]) back to the BSA. Air ambulance evacuation from the point of injury will be mission, enemy, terrain, troops, time available, and civilian considerations (METT-TC) dependent. Air ambulances from the corps or those positioned in the DSA will evacuate from the BSA to corps hospitals.

(6) The medical evacuation battalion communications link to the air ambulance company is accomplished by a combination of wire, frequency modulated (FM) voice, and mobile subscriber equipment (MSE). To enable air-to-air communications between medical evacuation aircraft and aviation brigade

aircraft during the conduct of missions, air ambulance companies obtain aviation unit call signs, frequencies, and cryptonet variables.

(7) Corps aeromedical elements will operate from the DSA and BSAs providing around the clock immediate response evacuation aircraft. To accomplish this, elements must maintain a close tie with the A2C2 system in the division. The division A2C2 element provides an airspace plan through the division operation order (OPORD)/OPLAN A2C2 annex. The aircrew must also be familiar with the daily airspace control order and the airspace control plan. These documents contain all airspace control measures (ACM), to include free fire areas, no-fly/fire areas, restricted operations zones, and established and standard Army aircraft flight routes (SAAFRs). These route and ACMs change on a daily basis and cannot be integrated into the division OPORD. The DSS will ensure all A2C2 information is provided to corps aeromedical elements. The DSS does not generate A2C2 information, but does provide A2C2 planning information to division A2C2 elements. This information includes, but is not limited to, the following:

- Locations of medical aviation and medical units.

- Locations of forward air refueling equipment.

- Locations of supported units and liaison requirements.

- Locations of evacuation corridors and recommendations on usage.

(8) All medical air-flight crews will communicate directly with the division air traffic service and execute division A2C2 while operating behind brigade boundaries. The medical evacuation battalion normally deploys air ambulance elements to the division. These elements include an air ambulance company or a selected element of the company. When the air ambulance company deploys to the division, it collocates with the aviation brigade, or according to the division TSOP. Air ambulance companies will obtain A2C2 information from the division A2C2 section and coordinate with the DSS. Air ambulance teams can be deployed forward into the BSA and collocate with the FSB. When deployed forward, the air ambulance team is totally dependent on the FSB for communications support. When air ambulance elements operate forward of the BSA, they will execute the A2C2 plan through the brigade S3. The FSB's support operations section provides planning and coordination between air evacuation elements and the maneuver brigade S3. Information provided to the maneuver brigade S3 should include, but not be limited to, the following:

- Location of MTFs and AXPs.

- Location and number of aircraft in sections.

- Location of AMEDD forward air refueling equipment.

- Locations of supported units and liaison requirements.

- Locations of evacuation corridors and recommendations on usage.

(9)   The brigade S3 provides the A2C2 plan which includes the air corridors, air control points, and communications checkpoints. The brigade S3 will provide updates as required.

1-9.   Interface with the Division Support Battalion

The DSS coordinates through the DISCOM medical operations branch, and interfaces with staff elements of the DSB on CHS issues pertaining to the DSA, and attachment/OPCON of corps medical elements. Interface with the division support medical company will primarily concern area medical support activities for the DSA. All medical issues are coordinated with the DSB HSSO who is located in the headquarters section. For further discussion on the DSB, see FM 63-21-1.

1-10.   Interface with the Forward Support Battalions

After coordination with the DISCOM medical operations branch, the DSS can interface with elements of the FSB through the CHS cell (HSSO) of the support operations section. This interface between the DSS and elements of the FSB is driven by CHS requirements in the forward areas. This information will assist the DSS in planning, coordinating, and managing division medical elements and resources in support of the battle. Communications and coordination between elements of the DSS, DISCOM support operations section and medical operations branch and the FSBs are essential for continuous CHS. The DSS will normally interface through the HSSO with the following FSB elements:

a.   *S2/S3.* The S2 or S3 advises and assists the FSB commander in planning, coordinating, and supervising the communications, operations, training, security, and intelligence functions of the battalion.

b.   *Support Operations Section.* The support operations section's mission includes DS supply, field services, DS maintenance, CHS, and limited transportation functions. The section must ensure that logistics and CHS to the supported units remain at a level consistent with the type of tactical operations being conducted. Interface between the support operations section and the DSS will be direct or indirect. The FSB HSSO is assigned to the support operations section.

c.   *Forward Support Medical Company.* The FSMC provides CHS for the brigade as well as area medical support for the brigade rear and BSA. Combat health support operations are coordinated by the DSS through the DISCOM with the BSS and the FSB (HSSO). The DSS tasks elements of the FSMC, through DISCOM support operations chain of command, to provide division-level CHS. The HSSO, FSMC commander, and brigade surgeon are the principal managers of the CHS assets assigned or attached to the brigade.

1-11.   Interface with the Maneuver Battalions

Medical platoons organic to the maneuver battalion provide Echelon I CHS for the battalion and area medical support in forward areas. Coordination is made with the medical platoons through the BSS.

Section IV. COMMAND POST SETUP AND COMMUNICATIONS

1-12. Command Post, Division Headquarters

The DSS, as an element of the division sustainment cell relocates and establishes itself as part of the division main command post (CP). The sustainment cell consists of several 5-ton expandable vans. These expandable vans house the assistant division commander for support (ADCS), DISCOM headquarters, and division and DISCOM CSS staffs. The ADCS conducts the rear fight from the sustainment cell. For sample setup of the division sustainment cell, see FM 63-2-2.

    a. Command posts are organized in many different ways to accomplish their missions. There are several options for setting up the division CPs. The division has changed to a main CP (tactical command post administrative center). The main CP combines all of the functions of the old division main and division rear CPs. For example of division CPs, see FM 71-100.

    b. The DSS's area is setup according to division TSOPs.

1-13. Information, Communications, and Digitization

Effective management and control of division CHS operations are dependent on the DSS's ability to communicate with division and corps elements. The use of the area common-user system (ACUS), digitization of all echelons of CHS communications, digitization of the battlefield distribution (BD) transportation assets and lastly, modular medical organization structure provides the DSS information needed to tailor and synchronize CHS. Through real-time situational awareness, the DSS anticipates, coordinates, and provides CHS for the division to include all units attached, DS, and OPCON to the division. Information and communications assets available to the DSS include are provided in Table 1-4.

Table 1-4. Information and Communications Assets Available to the Division Surgeon's Section

RADIO SETS AN/VRC 88F (1 EACH) AN/VRC 89F (1 EACH) AN/GRC 213 (2 EACH)	**TELEPHONES & FACSIMILE (FAX)** DIGITAL NONSECURE VOICE TELEPHONE (4 EACH) DIGITAL SECURE VOICE TELEPHONE (1 EACH) MSE FACSIMILE
ROUTERS TACTICAL LAND AREA NETWORKS LOCAL AREA NETWORK ROUTER	**COMPUTER SYSTEMS** COMBAT SERVICE SUPPORT CONTROL SYSTEM THEATER ARMY MEDICAL MANAGEMENT INFORMATION SYSTEM MEDICAL COMMUNICATIONS FOR COMBAT CASUALTY CARE THEATER MEDICAL INFORMATION PROGRAM
OTHERS WEATHER SYSTEM POSITION/NAVIGATION DEVICE (1 EACH)	FORCE XXI BATTLE COMMAND BRIGADE AND BELOW (3 EACH)

NOTE

Mobile subscriber equipment support for the DSS is
provided by elements of the division signal battalion.

a. Army Battle Command System. The primary means of communications within the digital division is through the use of the Army Battle Command System (ABCS). The DSS uses CSSCS to receive and transmit information and prepare briefings, overlays and plans. In addition, the DSS maintains an updated status of the tactical and logistics situations through the use of CSSCS. The division surgeon is responsible for establishing the CHS and CHL reporting procedures in the division using CSSCS and FBCB2. Complete details for use of the CSSCS at the CSSCS homepage @ http://www.lee.army.mil/CSSCS/.

b. Radio Communications Networks and Radios used by the DSS. Radio communications networks and radios used by the DSS include—

(1) The division logistics operations net (amplitude modulated [AM]—single sideband [SSB]) which is controlled by the DISCOM S2/S3 support operations section. The net provides the necessary long-range C2 link between the DISCOM, the FSBs, the DSB, the division materiel management center (DMMC) and the distribution management center (DMC) medical operations branch.

(2) The DSS maintains continual communications with division and DISCOM medical elements through its FM and AM radios. Single-Channel Ground and Airborne Radio System (SINCGARS) components provide the DSS with AN/VRC 89 series (FM) which has a receiver/transmitter capable of using two FM nets for reception and transmission. This permits the DSS to operate a medical net (FM). The DSS AM radio is an AN/GRC 213 radio (AM-improved high-frequency radio [IHFR]).

c. Mobile Subscriber Equipment. Mobile subscriber equipment is a part of the ACUS, which goes from the corps rear boundary forward to the division maneuver battalion's rear area. This system will allow the DSS to communicate throughout the battlefield in either a mobile or static situation. The mobile subscriber system is managed by the organic MSE signal battalion. The signal support company normally provides subscriber services to the division/DISCOM main CP. This system integrates the functions of transmission, switching, control, and terminal equipment. Additional information pertaining to MSE is found in FM 11-55 and FM 63-2-2.

(1) The MSE telephones, mobile subscriber radiotelephones (MSRTs), FAXs, data terminals, and computer systems, as part of the ACUS, are user-owned and operated. The DSS is responsible for running wire to the designated junction boxes. These boxes tie the DSS MSE telephones into the extension switches that access the system. The subscriber terminals used by the units are digital secure and nonsecure voice telephones. These provide full duplex digital, four-wire voice, as well as data ports, for interfacing the AN/UXC-7 FAX, the TACCS computer, and the unit-level computer (ULC). See FM 11-43 for information on how to connect the entry point terminal communications systems.

(2) Wire subscriber access points provide the entry points (interface) between fixed subscriber terminal equipment owned and operated by users and the MSE area system operated by signal units.

See FM 63-2-2 for information pertaining to fixed subscriber terminal equipment assignments for the DSS. The MSE MRST terminal is the AN/VRC-97. This MSRT, which consists of a very high-frequency radio and a digital secure voice terminal, is a vehicle-mounted assembly. It interfaces with the MSE system through a radio access unit (RAU). The primary use of the MSRT terminal is to provide mobile subscribers access to the MSE area network. Radio access units are deployed to maximize area coverage and MSRT terminal concentrations. Mobile subscriber radiotelephone terminals can also operate in CPs to allow staff and functional personnel access. Local standing operating procedures (SOP) will determine use of MSRTs in CP areas based on the possibility of interference with SINCGARS radios operating in the immediate area. As the Army continues to digitize the battlefield and modernize the force, the use of automation continues to develop.

(3) Mobile subscriber equipment Packet Switching Network gives units the ability to connect to division and corps tactical local area network (TACLAN). This allows units/CPs to connect computer systems such as the CSSCS and the maneuver control system, (MCS) to an ethernet cable (coaxial) and send and receive information in an extremely efficient manner. Packet switching does not utilize or take up existing telephone lines. Instead, telephone lines are freed up even more because information is being sent over a network on appliques. Using ABCS, common hardware/software facilitates the interface and exchange of information between the DSS, corps elements, and division medical elements. See FM 63-2-2 for information concerning automatic data processing (ADP) continuity of the OPLAN.

Section V. COMBAT HEALTH LOGISTICS AND BLOOD MANAGEMENT

1-14. Class VIII Resupply

a. Management. Class VIII resupply management in the Army XXI division is accomplished by medical units/elements through the use of a functional business system called Medical Logistics-Division (MEDLOG-D). Currently the functional business system for Class VIII wholesale/retail management at echelons above division (EAD) is the Theater Army Medical Management Information System (TAMMIS), which is a legacy system. This system will be replaced in the future by the Defense Medical Logistics Standard Support (DMLSS) System. Medical Logistics-Division is a module of DMLSS and is scheduled for fielding to division and corps medical units/elements. This system provides division and corps medical units/elements a direct link with the supporting MEDLOG battalion's units. The HSMO of the DSS and the DISCOM MMMB in the division support operations section coordinates Class VIII resupply for division medical units/elements. Each medical unit maintains its own basic load of 3 days of medical supplies. The MEDLOG battalion assigns one MEDLOG company in DS of each division. Once established, it provides Class VIII resupply for the division and corps medical elements operating in the division AO.

b. Resupply during (Employment and Initial) Employment.

(1) During deployment, lodgment, and early buildup phases, medical units operate from planned, prescribed loads and from existing pre-positioned war reserve stockpiles identified in applicable contingency plans.

(2) During the initial employment phase, each FSMC will receive a preconfigured medical resupply push-package every 48 hours from pre-positioned stock or the continental United States (CONUS) base. Preconfigured medical resupply push-packages will continue until appropriate units of the corps MEDLOG battalion are established.

(3) Initial resupply efforts will consist of preconfigured medical supply packages tailored to meet specific mission requirements. Preconfigured push-packages will normally be shipped directly to the division support medical company (DSMC) and FSMCs until replenishment line item requisitioning is established with the supporting MEDLOG company. During this time, medical company treatment and ambulance teams deployed with maneuver or other division elements are resupplied from their medical company. Maneuver battalion medical platoons/BAS will receive standard push-packages every 12 to 24 hours. Contents of push-packages can be adjusted as the battle changes. Line item requisitioning will be by exception only during this time. While resupply by preconfigured packages is intended to provide support during the initial phase, continuation on an exception only basis will be dictated by operational needs. Planning for such a contingency must be directly coordinated with the DSS. Other than line item requisitioning from the FSMCs and DSMC, the HSMO of the DSS and the DISCOM MMMB will coordinate all Class VIII requirements for the division with the supporting MEDLOG battalion and/or MEDLOG company, as appropriate.

c. *Medical Logistics-Division.* Divisional medical elements use MEDLOG-D to requisition Class VIII supplies. Users of this system in the division include maneuver battalion medical platoons, FSMCs, the DSMC, and the DISCOM MMMB. The MEDLOG-D system is the primary source for Class VIII line item requisitions from the FSMCs and DSMC. Forward support medical companies and the DSMC request Class VIII resupply from the supporting MEDLOG company.

d. *Routine Requisitions.* Routine requisitions from maneuver battalion medical platoons for Class VIII resupply from their supporting FSMC will be via a digital request. An information copy of all requisitions within the brigade will be forwarded by the FSMC on-line to the DISCOM MMMB and off-line to the BSS. Routine requisitions submitted by FSMCs, division or corps medical elements operating in the BSAs are forwarded directly to the supporting MEDLOG company. An information copy goes to the DISCOM MMMB. The MMMB coordinates shortfalls in throughput distribution with the DSS and divisions support operations branch. The MMMB updates priorities with the MEDLOG company to correct deficiencies in the delivery system. If the requested items are available for issue, a materiel release order is printed and the requested supplies are prepared for shipment. For items not available for issue, the requests are passed to the MEDLOG battalion's logistics support company. Using TAMMIS, the MEDLOG company forwards information to the unit on items shipped and on those requests which were not filled. An information copy is forwarded to the MMMB.

e. *Emergency Requisitions.* Emergency requisitions from maneuver battalion medical platoons are submitted to the supporting FSMC. When the supporting FSMC is unable to fill the request, the requisition is forwarded to the DISCOM MMMB. The DISCOM MMMB will expedite handling of this request to ensure tracking of critical Class VIII items and timely delivery. Cross-leveling in the division should be accomplished if it is the most expedient method of obtaining and shipping required items to the requesting unit/element. If the DISCOM MMMB is unable to locate requested item(s) in the division, the request is forwarded to the supporting MEDLOG company. Emergency requisitions from FSMCs are sent through the DISCOM MMMB for management and to ensure visibility of the requisitions. The DISCOM MMMB maintains a record of the requisition until it is filled. All emergency requests received by the MEDLOG company are processed for shipment by the most expedient transportation available. When feasible delivery of these emergency supplies are accomplished using air ambulances which is coordination with the medical evacuation battalion. The MEDLOG company immediately forwards all emergency requests not filled to the MEDLOG battalion logistics support company located in the corps rear. The DISCOM MMMB has the responsibility of monitoring all emergency requisitions not filled by the MEDLOG company. The DISCOM MMMB reports all emergency Class VIII requests to the DSS/CHS cell.

   f.   Delivery of Class VIII Supplies. Delivery of throughput Class VIII supplies to the requesting medical units in the division is accomplished by logistical packages (LOGPACs) and nonmedical transports. Shipment of these Class VIII LOGPACs from the MEDLOG company is coordinated with the corps support battalion and the corps MCO. The management and in-transit visibility of Class VIII delivery is accomplished through document number and transportation number tracking. The systems that work together to provide this management and coordination are TAMMIS, Transportation Coordinator's Automated Information for Movement System (TCAIMS), Movement Tracking System (MTS), and Global Traffic Network (GTN). These systems are located in the MEDLOG company and the DISCOM MMMB. In some cases, delivery of medical materiel into the division AO is achieved through use of the directed Class VIII resupply using medical evacuation resources that are returning to the division medical units. From the FSMCs, delivery of Class VIII supplies to maneuver battalion medical platoons via LOGPAC or nonmedical transports is coordinated by the FSMC with the FSB support operations section. For directed Class VIII resupply, medical transports can be used. Emergency Class VIII resupply will be processed for shipment by the most expedient means available. Based on casualty estimates, medical push-packages should be pre-positioned with maneuver battalion medical platoons or with the FSMC. Figure 1-2 provides an overview of Class VIII requisitions and resupply flow at Echelon I. Figure 1-3 provides an overview of Class VIII requisitions and resupply flow at Echelon II.

1-15.   Assemblage Management Reporting Under Unit Status Reporting

   a.   Unit Status Reporting. With the fielding of MEDLOG-D, unit status reporting (USR) of medical equipment sets (MES) in the division will be created using the MEDLOG-D USR feeder report. It calculates percentage fill of sets according to AR 220-1 and AR 40-61 and does not create a roll-up of equipment on-hand calculations. Minus the potency or dated items while units are not deployed, 70 percent fill of the combined expendable, durable, and nonexpendable items within a set constitute an on-hand set for accountability purposes. Medical equipment must be maintained at an acceptable degree of readiness to the level above 70 percent as determined by the division surgeon and unit commander. Division medical units/ elements will prepare a requisition plan to immediately replenish all potency, dated, and other items that are not being maintained and missing items from sets. Units will coordinate with the supporting MEDLOG company prior to implementation of the plan.

   b.   Transmission of Requisitions and Status Reports Data. Transmission of Class VIII requisitions and status reports data will be accomplished by one of a number of ways. The baseline method will always be by disk and hard copy. The preferred method will be by radio or MSE transmission if signal capabilities allow. At the battalion level, units will attempt to transmit requisition and report data using SINCGARS

Systems Improvement Program (SIP) or Enhanced Position Location Reporting System (EPLRS) linked to the hyperlink or modem capability of DMLSS-AM. Given the line of site limitations of FM radio, this attempt is best accomplished in synchronization with previously coordinated retransmission. Within the BSA and higher, transmission of data will be by either MSE or Harris radio (FM) if allowed. Note that if MSE is used, the unit must accomplish prior coordination with the division Assistant Chief of Staff (Signal) (G6) to obtain a net encryption system or other encryption hardware system in order to send data.

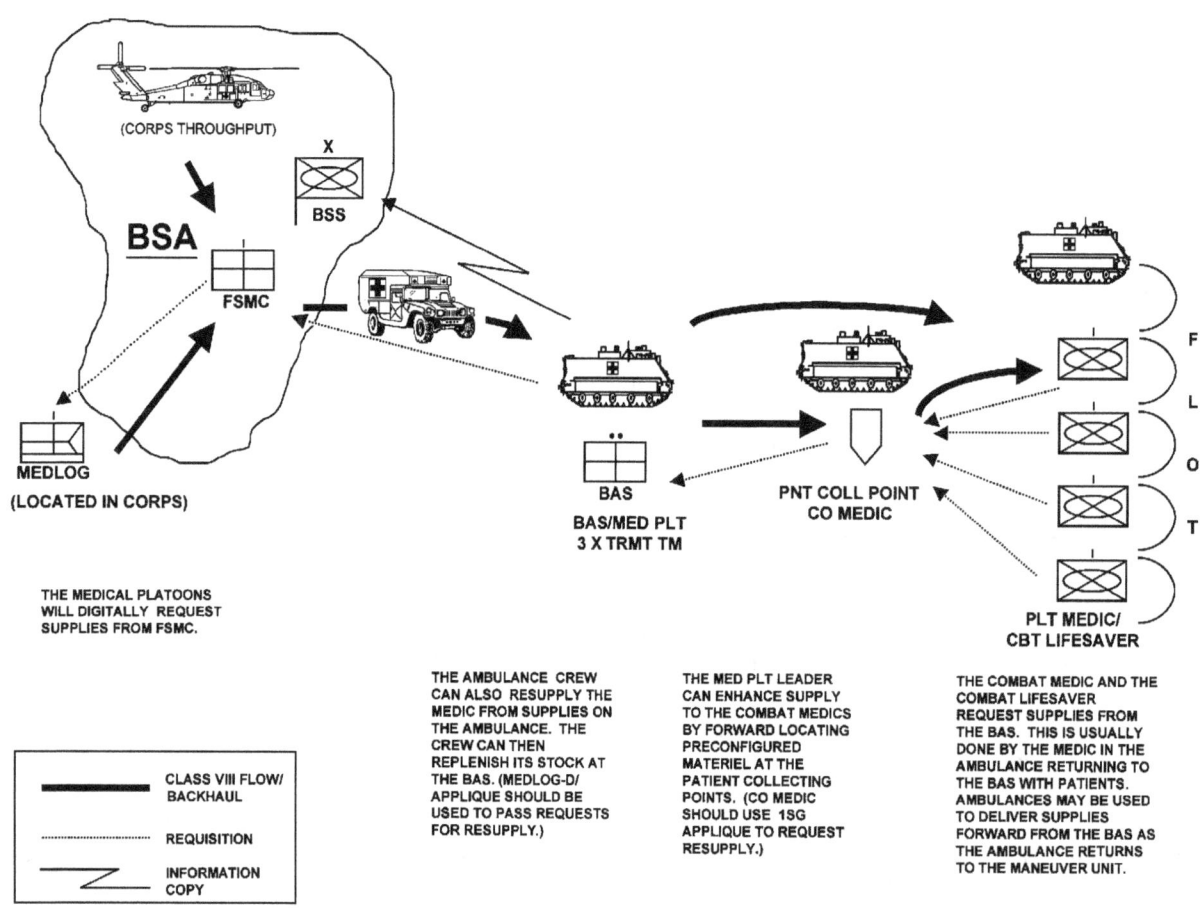

Figure 1-2. Overview of Class VIII resupply at Echelon I.

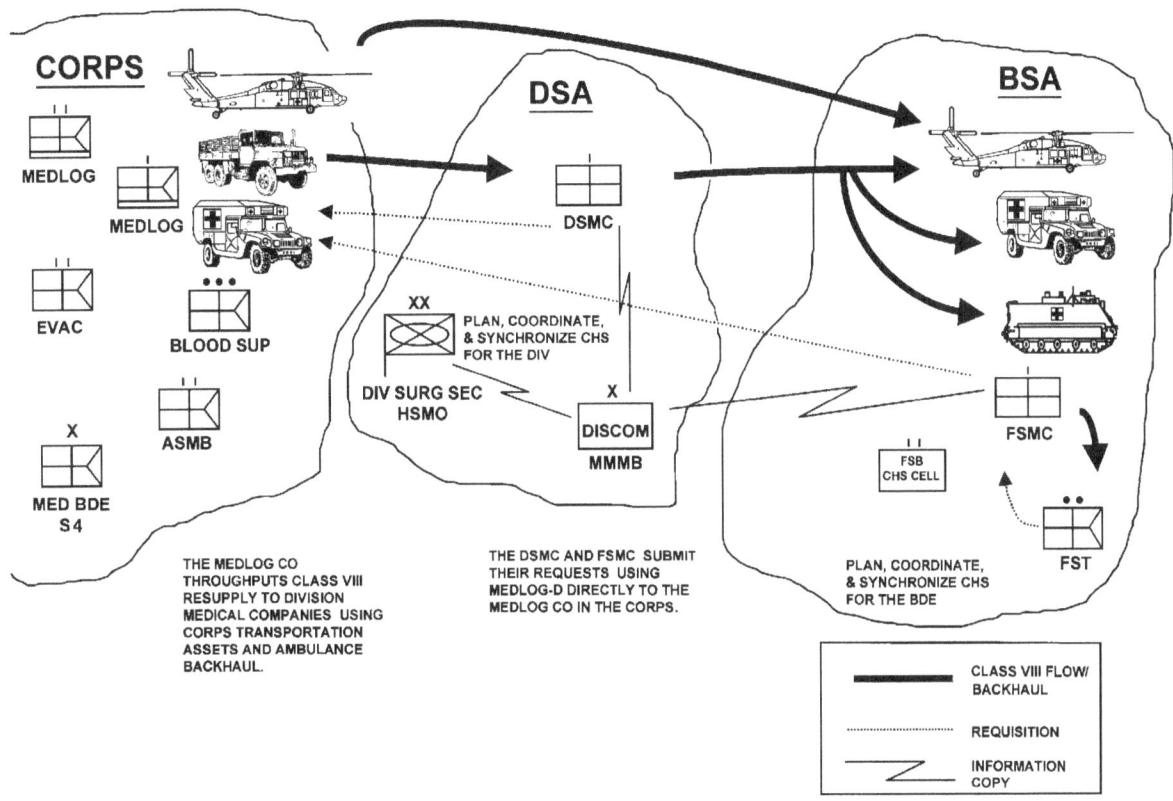

Figure 1-3. Overview of Class VIII resupply at Echelon II.

1-16. Medical Equipment Maintenance

The CHL Cell of the DSS will establish a list of critical medical equipment for the division. Units are to report the status of items on this list to the CHL cell.

 a. Medical Equipment Repairer. The medical equipment repairer provides operational and unit-level medical equipment maintenance for the FSMC and the brigade. He exercises his responsibilities by—

  • Scheduling and performing preventive maintenance checks and services (PMCS).

  • Performing electrical safety inspections and tests.

  • Accomplishing calibration, verification, and certification services.

  • Performing unscheduled maintenance functions with emphasis upon the replacement of assemblies, modules, and printed circuit boards.

- Operating a medical equipment repair parts program, to include Class VIII supplies as well as other commodity class parts.

- Maintaining a technical library of operator and maintenance technical manuals (TMs) and/or associated manufacturers' manuals (printed and/or digital).

- Conducting inspections for new or transferred equipment.

- Maintaining documentation of maintenance functions according to the provisions of Technical Bulletin (TB) 38-750-2 or DA standard automated system.

- Collecting and reporting data for readiness reportable medical equipment in accordance with AR 700-138.

- Requesting through the DISCOM, MMMB for maintenance support services, repairable exchange, or replacement from the Medical Standby Equipment Program (MEDSTEP), see AR 40-61.

b. *Mandatory Parts and Prescribed Load Lists.* Mandatory parts lists (MPLs) and prescribed load lists (PLLs) need to be monitored routinely. An MPL to support medical equipment is published annually in the Supply Bulletin (SB) 8-75 Series. Most medical equipment repair parts can be requisitioned through the Class VIII supply system; however, some repair parts are needed to repair medical equipment that falls in the category of Class IX repair parts (that is, common fasteners, electrical components, and others). Requisitions for Class IX repair parts are sent through the organization's supporting motor pool and require stringent monitoring and follow-up efforts. Special considerations for medical repair parts are explained in AR 40-61.

1-17. Division Blood Management

Blood requirements for the division are determined by the division surgeon. Only packed liquid red blood cells are expected to be available to the division. Blood products are shipped to Army MTFs in the division by the blood support detachment of the MEDLOG battalion. The DSS (HSMO) coordinates with the blood support detachment for division blood requirements.

a. *Blood Shipment.* Shipment of blood from the corps to the division is coordinated by the blood support detachment with the corps movement control center (CMCC). It is then transported to the requesting MTF by dedicated medical vehicles (air and ground). The blood support detachment notifies the DISCOM MMMB when blood is shipped. Emergency resupply can be accomplished by air ambulances from the medical battalion, evacuation or by medical personnel on nonstandard medical transports.

b. *Blood Support System.* Blood support is a combination of four systems (medical, technical, operational, and logistical). Blood support must be considered separate from laboratory support. In the long term, theater blood management is based on resupply from the CONUS donor bases (Armed Services Whole Blood Processing Laboratories [ASWBPLs]). At the corps level, storage and transportation refrigerators allow the blood support detachment to provide blood as far forward as the FSMCs of the division. See FMs 8-10, 8-10-9, 8-55, and TM 8-227-12 for definitive information on blood management.

CHAPTER 2

BRIGADE MEDICAL STAFF

Section I. BRIGADE SURGEON

2-1. Duties of the Brigade Surgeon

The brigade surgeon is an MC officer (Major, AOC 62BOO). He is a special staff officer who plans with and coordinates brigade CHS activities with the brigade S1. The brigade surgeon is assigned to the headquarters and headquarters company (HHC) of the maneuver brigade. The surgeon is responsible for the technical control of all medical activities in the command. The brigade surgeon oversees and coordinates CHS activities through the BSS and the brigade S3. The brigade surgeon keeps the brigade commander informed on the status of CHS for brigade operations and the health of the command. He provides input and obtains information to facilitate medical planning. His specific duties in this area include—

- Ensuring implementation of the CHS section of the brigade TSOP.

- Determining the allocation of medical resources within the brigade.

- Supervising technical training of medical personnel and the combat lifesaver program within the brigade.

- Determining procedures, techniques, and limitations in the conduct of routine medical care, emergency medical treatment (EMT), and advanced trauma management (ATM).

- Monitoring aeromedical and ground ambulance evacuation.

- Monitoring the implementation of automated medical systems.

- Informing the division surgeon on the brigade's CHS situation.

- Monitoring the health of the command and advising the commander on measures to counter disease and injury threats.

- Exercising technical supervision of subordinate battalion surgeons and PAs.

- Providing consultation and mentoring for subordinate battalion surgeon, physicians, and PAs.

- Providing the medical estimate and medical threat for inclusion in the commander's estimate.

2-2. Responsibilities of the Brigade Surgeon

The brigade surgeon, assisted by the BSS, is responsible for—

- Planning and coordinating the following CHS operations:

  - The system of treatment and medical evacuation (MEDEVAC), including aeromedical evacuation.

- Dental services.

- Preventive medicine services.

- Combat stress control.

- Medical supply and medical maintenance support, including technical inspection and status reports.

- Medical humanitarian assistance (see FM 8-42 pertaining to Title 10, United States Code requirements).

- Combat health support within the command.

- Preparation of reports regarding medical administrative records of injured, sick, and wounded personnel.

- Advising on health status of the command and of the occupied or friendly territory within the commander's area of responsibility.

- Reviewing all brigade OPLANs and contingency plans to identify potential medical hazards associated with geographical locations and climatic conditions.

- Advising on the medical effects of the environment, NBC, and directed-energy devices on personnel, rations, and water.

- Identifying and tracking critical Class VIII items and establishing priorities for procurement.

- Determining requirements for medical personnel and making recommendations concerning their assignments.

- Coordinating with the FSB HSSO and maneuver battalion staff elements for continuous CHS.

- Submitting to higher headquarters those recommendations on professional medical problems that require research and development.

- Providing recommendations on allocation and redistribution of AMEDD personnel, CHL, and CHS during the reconstitution process.

- Advising commanders about the PVNTMED aspects of all operations and the availability and use of CSC teams.

- Advising commanders on the effects of accumulated fatigue, radiation exposure, possible delayed effects from exposure to chemical or biological agents, and use of countermeasures and pretreatments.

• Advising commanders on policy for personnel exposed to lethal but not immediately life-threatening doses of radiation or chemical and biological agents.

• Ensuring that clear and accurate patient records are maintained of all clinical encounters for supported deployed personnel through the use of a DA Form 8007-R or through the use of digital patient records, as they become available. See AR 40-66 and FM 8-10-1 for management of individual health records in the field. Also, digital patient records at the division and brigade level will be available through the fielding of MC4 and the TMIP.

Section II. ORGANIZATION AND FUNCTIONS OF THE BRIGADE SURGEON'S SECTION

2-3.   Mission of the Brigade Surgeon's Section

The mission of the BSS is to plan, coordinate, and synchronize the brigade's CHS under the supervision of the brigade surgeon. An overview of the process for developing the OPLAN/OPORD is provided in Chapter 3. For definitive information on developing the OPLAN/OPORD, see FM 101-5.

2-4.   Responsibilities and Functions of the Brigade Surgeon's Section

a.   The BSS is assigned to the HHC of the brigade and operates out of the brigade TOC. The section, in coordination with the HSSO of the FSB support operations section and the FSMC commander, is responsible for the development of the medical portion of the brigade OPLAN/OPORD and takes part in the brigade planning process. The BSS staff is responsible to the brigade commander for staff supervision of CHS within the brigade. The BSS is also responsible for coordinating GS and DS relationships of organic medical units and medical units/elements whether under OPCON or attached to the brigade. The brigade commander is updated as required on the status of CHS in the brigade.

b.   Figure 2-1 shows the typical organization and staffing of the BSS. It consists of a medical plans and operations cell and a patient disposition and reports cell.

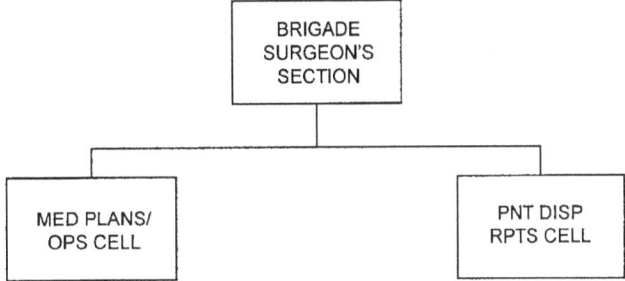

Figure 2-1. Brigade surgeon's section.

The staff of the BSS assists the brigade surgeon in planning and conducting brigade CHS operations. Specific functions of the BSS include—

- Planning and ensuring that Echelons I and II CHS for the brigade are provided in a timely and efficient manner.

- Planning and coordinating CHS operations for brigade medical assets, attached, or OPCON corps assets. This includes reinforcement and reconstitution.

- Coordinating with the DISCOM support operations section, the DISCOM medical operations branch, and the FSB support operations CHS cell (HSSO) for prioritizing the reallocation of organic and corps medical augmentation assets as required by the tactical situation.

- Ensuring that the medical annex of the brigade TSOPs, plans, policies, and procedures for CHS, prescribed by the brigade surgeon, are prepared and executed.

- Overseeing medical training and providing information to the brigade surgeon and brigade commander.

- Coordinating and prioritizing CHL and blood management requirements for the brigade.

- Collecting medical threat information and coordinating combat health intelligence requirements with the brigade S2 according to FM 8-10-8.

- Coordinating and directing patient evacuation from forward areas to supporting MTFs.

- Coordinating the MEDEVAC of all EPW casualties from the brigade AO.

- Coordinating the disposition of captured medical materiel.

- Coordinating, planning, and prioritizing PVNTMED missions.

- Coordinating with the supporting veterinary element for subsistence and animal disease surveillance.

2-5. Medical Plans and Operations Cell

The medical plans and operations cell is typically staffed with a—

- Medical plans officer.

- Medical operations sergeant.

- Medical operations/intelligence NCO.

This cell is responsible for—

- Developing CHS staff estimates for supporting brigade operations.

- Developing and coordinating the medical brigade CHS plan with the brigade staff, FSB, FSMC, and maneuver battalion medical platoons.

- Developing the CHS annex of the brigade OPLAN/OPORD.

- Overseeing and synchronizing brigade CHS operations.

- Monitoring medical troop strength to determine task organization for mission accomplishment.

- Forwarding all medical information of potential intelligence value to the brigade S2 and S3 sections.

- Obtaining updated medical threat and intelligence information through the brigade S2 and S3 sections and from the DSS for evaluation and applicability.

- Coordinating the disposition of captured medical materiels according to the TSOPs.

- Coordinating through the DSS for corps medical support reinforcement/augmentation, as required.

- Verifying emergency supply requests and taking the necessary action to expedite delivery.

- Monitoring Class VIII resupply levels to ensure adequate stockage for support of brigade operations.

- Tracking and managing critical Class VIII items in coordination with the maneuver battalion medical platoons, FSMC, DSS and brigade surgeons.

2-6. Patient Disposition and Reports Cell

The patient disposition and reports cell assists the operations officer with tracking patient disposition of brigade personnel. This cell prepares and forwards appropriate patient statistical reports to the division headquarters according to the division TSOP.

2-7. Information and Communications

a. The Brigade Surgeon's Section Communications and Information Systems. Information and communications assets available to the BSS include radio sets (AN/VRC 89 series [FM]); digital nonsecure voice telephone (1 each); MSE FAX; TACLAN work station (WS); local area network (LAN) router;

MCS; CSSCS; and FBCB2/position/navigation (1 each). The BSS has a CSSCS that aids the BSS with maintaining real-time situational awareness and understanding of what is happening on the battlefield. This system tracks unit information down to the company level. Included in the classes of supplies tracked by the CSSCS is Class VIII. Using the CSSCS to track Class VIII will enhance the BSS's ability to identify critical Class VIII items. The BSS will exchange information with the FSMC, the DSMC, and the DSS, using the CSSCS. For definitive information on the CSSCS, see FMs 63-20-1, 63-21-1, and 63-23-2.

   b.   *Combat Health Support Functions on Force XXI Battle Command Brigade and Below System.* The FBCB2 is a hardware/software suite that digitizes C2 at brigade and below level. The FBCB2 system provides a seamless battle command capability for performance of missions throughout the operational continuum at the tactical level. The FBCB2 system is the implementation of information technology to provide increased battlefield operational capabilities. The system is positioned on specified platforms and will perform combat, combat support (CS) and CSS functions for the planning and execution of operations. This system gives the BSS a common relevant picture of the current CHS situation at BAS, AXPs, and the FSMC. For the first time, the medical organizations and elements are digitally linked to the platforms and organizations they support. The current CSS functionality on FBCB2 gives the combatant a common relevant picture of the current CSS situation at his echelon of command and at subordinate levels. It also provides the personnel and logistics leaders CSS situational awareness and understanding throughout their battle space. It also provides enhanced capability to synchronize support to customer units. Combat service support functionally on FBCB2 includes the following:

   • Logistics situation report (LOGSITREP).

   • Personnel situation report (PERSITREP).

   • Medical situation report.

   • Situation awareness.

   • Logistics call for support.

   • Logistics task order.

Currently the FBCB2 also permits information to be entered using free text such as comments and other pertinent CSS information. This common battle space picture will enable CHS providers to maintain the operational tempo set by the maneuver commander. There are three medical screens incorporated into the CSS applique function. They are the medical functionality in the LOGSITREP, the MEDSITREP, and the MEDEVAC request. It is important that units use standard message and reports formats to eliminate confusion. As the system is further developed and additional CHS screens are added, there will be less space for using free text. Figure 2-2 is the medical screen as seen on the CSS function of FBCB2. Descriptions of each screen are provided below.

   (1)   *Medical functionality in the logistics situation report.* This message provides visibility of selected Class VIII items at the BAS and FSMC levels, date-time group (DTG) of the most recent report, and location of medical units. Recipients of the report are the forward support company (FSC), the

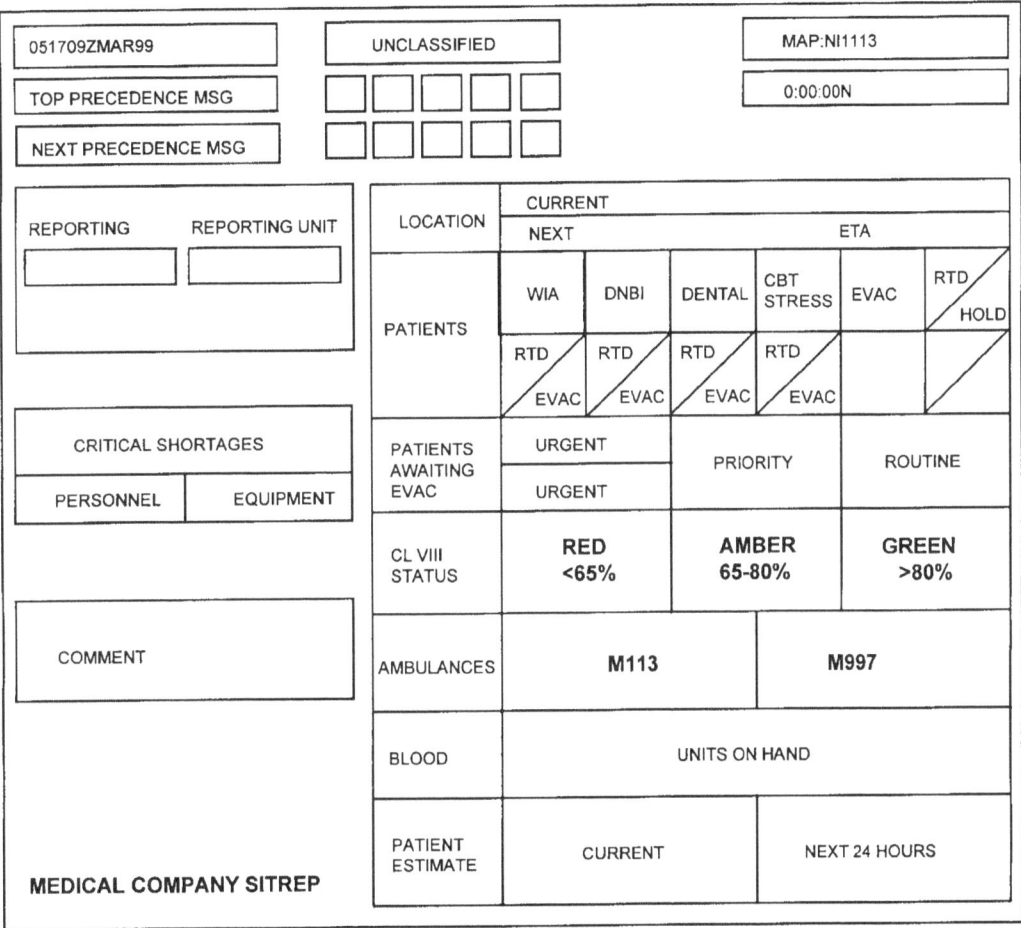

Figure 2-2. Sample of medical screen incorporated into the combat service support Force XXI Battle Command Brigade and Below function.

FSB support operations (HSSO), the BSS, and the DSS. This report does not replace TAMMIS; however, it is entered into CSSCS by the BSS.

(2) *Medical situation report.* The FSMC and BAS prepare and submit this report. The recipients of the report are maneuver commanders and their S1, the FSCs, the FSB support operations (HSSO), the FSMC, the BSS, and the DSS. The BSS and FSMC receive roll up from the BAS. The DSS receives a roll up of the FSMC reports. Adjacent units can receive information copies of the MEDSITREP. This message reports the following information:

(*a*) Current location and proposed next location with estimated time of arrival (ETA).

(*b*) Number of patients seen and classified as wounded in action (WIA), DNBI, dental, and combat stress. The field will also show the number of patients evacuated and the number returned to duty (RTD).

(*c*)   Patient(s) awaiting MEDEVAC.

(*d*)   The Class VIII status of the element/unit, the number of ambulances that are mission capable, and the number of units of blood and type on hand.

(*e*)   Free text field for critical Class VIII or other supply shortages and commander's comments.

(3)   *Medical evacuation request.* This request is currently embedded into the FBCB2 and is a digitized standard 9-line MEDEVAC request. The current messaging is from the requestor to the medical platoon leader (with an information copy to the maneuver battalion commander). The medical platoon leader either responds or forwards the request to the FSMC commander who dispatches the appropriate MEDEVAC asset. Information copies of all MEDEVAC requests are sent to the BSS so they can maintain real-time situation awareness on the volume of requests. The FSMC commander sends an information copy to the BSS with after-action information that includes destination of evacuated patient(s).

c.   *Radio Nets.* Radio nets used by the BSS include—

(1)   The division logistics operations net (AM-SSB), which is controlled by the DISCOM S2/ S3 support operations section. The net provides the necessary long-range C2 link between the DISCOM, the FSBs, the DSB, and the DMMC.

(2)   The BSS maintains communication with medical elements supporting the brigade through its FM medical net. Single-channel ground and airborne radio system components provide the BSS with an AN/VRC 89 series (FM) which has a receiver/transmitter (R/T) capable of using two FM nets for reception and transmission. This permits the BSS to communicate with CHS elements via the administrative/logistic net (FM). The AN/VRC-89 series has two R/Ts (and one power amplifier). The two R/Ts allow the BSS to participate in two FM nets. These nets include the brigade administrative/logistics net and one of the three medical platoons operations nets. The BSS also communicates using AM-IHFR with its AN/GRC 213 or AN/GRC 193A radio. Another technique is to use the FSMC command net for brigadewide medical communications while using the administrative/logistics net for other CSS integration. Situation awareness is monitored using FBCB2 and by face-to-face contact with other brigade staff members in the brigade TOC.

d.   *Mobile Subscriber Equipment.* Mobile subscriber equipment will allow the BSS to communicate throughout the battlefield in either a mobile or static situation. As the Army continues to digitize the battlefield and modernize the force, the use of automation continues to develop. Mobile subscriber equipment packet switching network gives units the ability to connect to division and corps LANs or wide area network (WAN). A WAN is similar to the LAN but covers a larger distance. This allows units/CPs to connect computer systems such as the CSSCS, MCS, and FBCB2 to an ethernet cable (coaxial) and send and receive information in an extremely efficient manner. Because of the limitations of a network constructed with coaxial cable, a WAN uses a combination of the MSE packet switch network and radio networks to distribute the data where necessary through the system. Packet switching does not use or take up existing telephone lines. Instead, telephone lines are freed up even more because information is being sent over a network on computers and related equipment. Using the common hardware/software facilitates the interface and exchange of information between the BSS, medical platoons operating BAS, FSMCs, DSS, corps, and division medical elements. See FM 63-2-2 for information concerning ADP continuity of the operations plan.

   e. Combat Service Support Control System. The CSSCS is the CSS component of ABCS. This is the primary CSS information tool used within the DISCOM. The CSSCS provides a concise picture of unit requirements and support capabilities by collecting, processing, and displaying information on key items of supplies, services, and personnel that the commanders deem crucial to the success of an operation. The CSSCS does not duplicate Standard Army Management Information System (STAMIS) functions. The management of all items within a class of supply or support functions remains STAMIS functions. Items tracked in CSSCS represent a small, but critical portion of the items managed by STAMIS. The CSSCS also supports the decision-making process with course of action (COA) analysis. Staffs can analyze up to three COA for a 4-day period. Variables include combat intensity, combat posture, unit task organization, miles traveled, and geographical region. This system maintains a database of unit personnel and equipment authorizations by standard requirements code (SRC) (similar to table of organization and equipment [TOE]) and unit and equipment planning factors. It includes a database of equipment and personnel called a baseline resource item list (BRIL). The items that a commander identifies as critical to the operation can be selected from the BRIL to establish the CTIL. The CSSCS currently provides situation awareness of critical elements within supply Classes I, II/IV, IIIB, IIIP, V, VII, and VIII, and personnel strength management. Maintenance, transportation, and medical functionality are a few features to be added as the system matures.

   (1) *Data collection on the combat service support control system.* Unit supply status and requirements can be entered manually using standard input forms (screens) at the brigade S4, DSB, DASB, or FSB CSSCS terminal. Electronic interfaces to systems such as the FBCB2 will greatly enhance the entry of unit data. The CSSCS tracks unit information down to the company level. Battle loss spot reports can be inputted to the CSSCS node at any level (brigade, division, or corps). Information is entered either manually, as in the case of Class III, or by electronic transfer as when a STAMIS disk is downloaded into the CSSCS terminal. The CSSCS automatically updates the database. The data is then distributed to other CSSCS nodes. The primary means of communication is MSE. The CSSCS nodes then manipulate the data through a series of algorithms that are based on Army planning factors, the specified task organization, and the established support relationships. This way, large quantities of data are presented in comprehensive, but usable, decision support information formats. This information is graphically portrayed to the commander through green, amber, red, and black bubble charts; situational awareness; subordinate unit locations; and supply point status. Status can be projected out to 4 days using a combination of planning factors and manually generated estimates. The commander and his staff can further evaluate simplified color status by accessing more detailed numerical data that supports the color status displayed. At the divisional brigade level, two CSSCS devices (or nodes) will exist. One is located in the brigade S1 and S4 operational facility and the other in the FSB support operations section. The brigade node is the point of entry into the CSSCS for all organizational-level CSS status and requirements of the brigade and its subordinate units. The brigade S1/S4 can also view the status of its supporting FSB/DASB and higher echelon supply points. Through interfaces to the other Army Tactical Command and Control System (ATCCS), a CSSCS node provides the brigade S1/S4 with the battlefield common picture. The FSB, DASB, and DSB CSSCS node serves as the entry point for some supply point data that is not supported by a STAMIS and all organizational status of their elements. The FSB, DASB, and DSB use CSSCS to—

- Track and anticipate customer logistic status and requirements.

- Track supply point status, issues, receipts, and due-ins of CTIL items.

(2) *Combat service support control system interfaces.* All CSSCS nodes will be able to interface with all other CSSCS devices and are also able to interface with other ATCCS such as air missile defense workstations (AMDWS), MCS, all source analysis system, and Advanced Field Artillery Tactical Data System (AFATDS). The CSSCS connects to the FBCB2 at the brigade S1/S4 level. The FBCB2 will serve as a data source for CSSCS by passing aggregate data (MEDSITREP, LOGSITREP, and PERSITREP) that has been rolled up from squad/section, platoon, company, and battalion. The LOGSITREP includes roll-ups of Classes I, IIIP, IIIB, IV, V, VII, and VIII. Class VII data also includes nonmission capable information. The CSSCS consolidates battalion data selected by the commander on the CTIL, up to 120 items. The CSSCS reports to higher headquarters and then provides the lower echelons with the location of supply points via FBCB2. Force XXI Battle Command Brigade and Below transmits personnel strength information by officer/warrant officer/enlisted through the PERSITREP. This information is rolled up from platform through battalion to brigade S1 where it is entered directly into CSSCS or the Army XXI manning system resident on the CSSCS. The CSSCS uses this information to update its database on those personnel categories listed on the CTIL. The CSSCS updates supply point locations whenever supply points moves an electronic map overlay format and passes it down to platform level via FBCB2.

2-8. Medical Standard Army Management Information System

The MC4 system will be a theater automated CHS system, which links commanders, health care providers, and supporting elements, at all echelons, with integrated medical information. The system provides digital enablers to connect, both vertically and horizontally, all ten CHS functional business systems. The MC4 system receives, stores, processes, transmits, and reports medical C2, medical surveillance, casualty movement/tracking, medical treatment, medical situational awareness, and MEDLOG data across all levels of care. This will be achieved through the integration of a suite of medical information systems linked through the Army data telecommunications architecture. The MC4 system begins with the individual soldier and continues throughout the health care continuum. The best way to visualize the MC4 system capability is as a piece of the Army digital computer network where all ten CHS functional areas have been digitized and the CHS information made available to specified commands, supported units, and their personnel. Not only will the MC4 system provide the Army commanders with CHS information, but will provide him with a seamless transition to the joint CHS environment.

a. Components of Medical Communications for Combat Casualty Care System. The MC4 system will consist of three basic components: software, hardware, and telecommunications capabilities.

(1) *Software capability.*

(*a*) The joint TMIP will provide government off-the-shelf (GOTS)/commercial off-the-shelf (COTS) software and interoperability standards to support joint theater operations. The software provides an integrated medical information capability that will support all levels of care in a TO with links to the sustaining base. Medical capabilities provided by the software to support commanders in the theater will address medical C2 (including medical capability assessment, sustainability analysis, and medical intelligence); MEDLOG (including blood product management and medical maintenance management); casualty evacuation; and health care delivery.

(*b*) The MC4 system will support Army-unique requirements and any software needed to interface with Army information systems such as CSSCS, Global Command and Control System-Army (GCCS-A), FBCB2, Warrior Programs, and the MTS.

(2) *Hardware capability.* The hardware capability will consist of COTS automation equipment supporting the above software capabilities. Examples include, but are not limited to, computers, printers, networking devices, and the personal information carrier (PIC).

(3) *Telecommunications capability.* The MC4 capability will rely on current and proposed Army solutions for tactical, operational, and strategic telecommunications systems to transmit and receive digitized medical information throughout the theater and back to the sustaining base. There will be no separate AMEDD communication system. Telecommunications at brigade and below will be accomplished through the tactical internet; above brigade level, telecommunications will be accomplished through the warfighter information network (WIN) architecture. The MC4 system will include hardware or software required to interface with current and emerging technologies supporting manual, wired, and wireless data transmission. At end-state, the MC4 system users will exchange data electronically via the WIN architecture. In the interim, commercial satellite and/or high-frequency radios will be fielded to selected medical units (for example, medical detachment-telemedicine [MDT]) receiving the MC4 system to support high band-width requirements until the WIN architecture is fully fielded. Personnel operating satellite assets are resourced in the MDT TOE and will be located with the MDT.

b. *Patient Treatment Recording System.* Under the MC4 system, medical information about each soldier will be entered into a local database maintained at the supporting BAS or troop medical clinic. This information will include the soldier's immunization status, medical deployability status, and dental deployability status. A commander, faced with a deployment, will be able to simply query the database to gain the deployability status of the entire command. Time previously spent on physically searching paper records will be available for other tasks. Under the MC4 system each soldier will be issued a PIC. The PIC is an electronic device that will store personal information about the individual soldier. The PIC specifications are addressed in a separate DOD requirements document, which incorporates Army operational requirements into this standard joint device. The PIC will be used to record all of the soldier's health care events and the soldier's readiness status. Each time a soldier receives medical care or immunizations, the medical history on the PIC will be updated. When a soldier is deployed, his PIC will contain baseline clinical data. During processing for deployment, the medical staff will be able to read all immunizations, medical and dental patient history data directly from the PIC, speeding up the process. Once in an operational theater, the soldier's PIC will continue to provide a backup record of all medical events that occur during the deployment. Any medical data generated by a medical event will be entered onto the PIC as well as being entered into the MC4 information system. The preservation of medical data will no longer rely on safeguarding and transporting stacks of paper records.

CHAPTER 3

DIVISION AND BRIGADE COMBAT HEALTH SUPPORT OPERATIONS

Section I. PLANNING COMBAT HEALTH SUPPORT FOR DIVISION AND BRIGADE OPERATIONS

3-1. Division Combat Health Support Planning

  a. Division CHS operations involve all of the factors that must be considered in the initial developmental stages of the division CHS plan. The CHS plan is updated to meet tactical or CHS operations requirements. The following factors should be considered:

- Information requirements (current task organization structure, medical troop strengths, projected weather and environmental factors, and maintenance status of medical equipment).

- Results of the mission analysis.

- Commander's intent.

- Planning guidance.

- Courses of actions.

- Tactical plan.

- Enemy.

- Terrain.

- Troops.

- Weather.

- Threat (including medical threat).

- Operational conditions and constraints.

- Military population supported.

- Civilian populace in the AO.

- Medical personnel status.

- Equipment status of medical units and elements.

- Supply status including Class VIII.

- Wartime HN support.

- Indigenous medical services.

- Communications capability.

- Nuclear, biological, and chemical defense including OEG.

- Nuclear, biological, and chemical casualty considerations.

- Training status.

- Casualty estimates.

- Medical evacuation requirements and capabilities.

- Corps CHS status.

- Nonmedical support requirements from division.

- Area support requirements.

- Special operations support requirements.

- Army airspace command and control.

- Medical records and reports requirements.

- Phases of operations.

- Allied/coalition health assets requirements.

- Policy and procedure updates.

b. The division CHS plan is developed by the DSS staff with assistance from the DISCOM medical staff. See FMs 8-10, 8-10-6, 8-10-8, 8-10-9, 8-42, 8-55, 63-2-2, 63-20-1, 63-21-1, 63-23-2, 100-5 and 101-5 for doctrinal guidance on CHS operations. After the CHS plan is completed, it is incorporated into the CSS plan. After the CSS and other areas of the division plan are approved by the division commander, it is incorporated into the division OPORD.

3-2. Division Operation Plan and Operation Order

The G3 section, using input from each of the staff elements of the division headquarters, develops the division OPLAN and OPORD.

NOTE

An approved plan becomes an order.

a. The division surgeon is responsible for supervision and development of CHS input for the division OPORD. The division CHS plan serves as the base document for this input. The division CHS plan is revised or updated based on mission analysis or changes in CHS requirements. The division surgeon is tasked by the G3 for CHS input to the division OPORD for support of division operations. The G3 indicates time-line requirements. The division surgeon is involved in all stages of the planning process. He and his staff participate in all phases of the planning process. This allows them to identify all CHS requirements. Information for development of staff estimates and the OPLAN/OPORD are discussed below.

b. The medical plan/operations cell develops a CHS plan based on guidance received from the division commander and the division surgeon. The DSS provides CHS operational planning updates to the division surgeon. The CHS plan is briefed to the division commander for approval, as required. The CHS plan is provided to the G3 according to the format of the CHS outline in FM 8-55.

c. The DSS has a primary responsibility for the coordination of division and corps medical assets in support of the division. Supporting medical elements should be pre-positioned according to the CHS plan and anticipated requirements. Division and corps evacuation assets should be task-organized to support the area of greatest casualty density. All supporting medical elements should be issued the maximum allowable levels of Class VIII and other required supplies. The DSS must establish and maintain continuous communications with the DISCOM medical operations branch and the BSS. The DISCOM medical operations branch and the BSS maintain continuous communication with the DSB and FSB HSSOs. The medical plan/operations cell maintains a situational map that includes overlays with friendly, as well as threat information. The cell should use charts to monitor functional areas. Subject areas that could enhance situational awareness or mission areas that are critical to CHS operations should be tracked. In digitized units, situational awareness will be maintained using the CSSCS modules for locations of friendly units, corps ground and air ambulance assets, and all other areas listed below which are normally maintained on a situational map. For digitized units the traditional situational map is only maintained as a back up to the ATCCS and programs. The subject areas that are to be tracked should be identified by the division surgeon and/or the chief medical planner and may include—

- Corps ground and air ambulance assets.

- Army airspace command and control overlays.

- Threat picture (includes tracking reports and posting updates so that the threat is portrayed on the situational map).

- Current routes and their status.

- Maintenance status of evacuation platforms.

- Status of units operating in high-risk environments or with threat/enemy contact.

- Division to corps evacuation schedule and evacuation delays.

- Supply status including critical Class VIII shortages.

- Critical medical personnel and equipment shortages.

- Pending resupply missions from corps.

- Medical maintenance backlog.

- Patient status board (for example, awaiting evacuation from division to corps).

- Hospitals supporting the division with latest bed spaces available, additional/shortages of specialties, and locations (this is a division-level requirement, except for some stability operations or support operations).

- Blood status.

- Dirty routes and patient decontamination sites.

- Brigade operations and CSS overlays.

3-3. Brigade Combat Health Support Planning

Brigade CHS planning is accomplished based on the same factors found in division CHS planning. The brigade surgeon is responsible for development of the brigade CHS plan. He tasks the BSS with development of the brigade CHS plan. The brigade plan/operations cell has the primary responsible for developing and coordinating the brigade CHS plan. The foundation of the brigade CHS plan is the brigade commander's guidance and the division CHS plan.

3-4. Brigade Operation Plan and Operation Order

Planning starts with mission analysis. The brigade begins mission analysis when the division provides enough information for the brigade staff to analyze. Mission analysis is done by the entire brigade staff and is an integral part of the planning for an operation. Information that the brigade staff analyzes will normally be provided with a well-written warning order (WARNO) or after receiving several WARNOs from the division. The first WARNO from the brigade should be issued as soon as possible after receiving the division WARNO for a new operation. The mission analysis (see Table 3-1) is Step 1 of the military decision-making process (MDMP). See FM 101-5 for further discussion on the MDMP. For guidance on military decision making in abbreviated planning for a time-constrained situation, see Center for Army

Lessons Learned Newsletter, Number 99-12 Update, located at http://call.army.mil/call/homepage/ newsltr.htm. The BSS must ensure all available CHS information is included in the brigade WARNO. The BSS could also forward additional coordinating instructions down to the medical platoon level. These coordinating instructions are normally transmitted in a force text E-mail message via the TACLAN. As part of the mission analysis and based on the brigade commander's intent and guidance, the BSS develops CHS staff estimates for supporting brigade operations. An understanding of the brigade combat teams (BCT) time lines or battle rhythm will assist the medical planner in developing the CHS input to the brigade OPLAN/OPORD. Bear in mind that parallel planning is occurring at different levels of command; for example, the brigade WARNO allows the subordinate unit to begin their planning process, allowing maximum use of the available time for planning. Timely WARNOs are the key to effective parallel planning. When decisions are made or pertinent information becomes available, the brigade staff issues WARNOs as a part of the planning process. See Chapter 5 and Appendix H of FM 101-5 for additional information on WARNOs. Mission analysis includes—

- Assessing CHS capabilities (organic and attached assets with current status and location).

- Assessing limitations for CHS assets that are not available, specify reason.

- Identifying specified, implied, and essential CHS tasks in the division OPORD.

The following is an example of subject areas that should be addressed during mission analysis:

- Treatment (to include surgical requirements).

- Emergency and sustaining dental treatment.

- Patient holding.

- Combat stress control.

- Preventive medicine.

- Medical evacuation support by air and ground ambulances (and nonmedical evacuation platforms, if necessary).

- Class VIII resupply and blood support.

- Medical maintenance.

- Nuclear, biological, and chemical operations.

- The threat to treatment and evacuation assets capable of causing CHS failure.

- Likely targeted area of threat chemical weapons strike and types of agents (the S2 and the chemical officer should brief the BSS on the effects possible requirement).

- Casualty estimates (number and types of casualties).

- Terrain effects on evacuation.

- Current medical status of brigade personnel.

Table 3-1. Mission Analysis of the Situation

---

1. **MISSION ANALYSIS**
   A. MISSION AND INTENT OF COMMANDER TWO LEVELS UP.
   B. MISSION AND INTENT OF IMMEDIATE COMMANDER.
   C. ASSIGNED TASKS (SPECIFIED AND IMPLIED).
   D. CONSTRAINTS AND LIMITATIONS.
   E. MISSION-ESSENTIAL TASKS.
   F. RESTATED MISSION.
   G. TENTATIVE TIME SCHEDULE.

2. **ESTIMATE THE SITUATION AND DETERMINE COURSES OF ACTION**
   A. TERRAIN AND WEATHER.
      (1) TERRAIN—OBSERVATION AND FIELDS OF FIRE, CONCEALMENT AND COVER, OBSTACLES, KEY TERRAIN, AND AVENUES OF APPROACH (OCOKA).
      (2) WEATHER—VISIBILITY, MOBILITY, SURVIVABILITY.
   B. ENEMY SITUATION AND COA.
      (1) COMPOSITION.
      (2) DISPOSITION.
      (3) RECENT ACTIVITIES.
      (4) CAPABILITIES.
      (5) WEAKNESS.
      (6) MOST PROBABLE COA (ENEMY USE OF METT-TC)
      (7) MOST DANGEROUS COA.
   C. FRIENDLY SITUATION—METT-TC.
   D. FRIENDLY COA. DEVELOP A MINIMUM OF TWO.

3. **ANALYSIS OF COURSES OF ACTION**
   A. SIGNIFICANT FACTORS.
   B. WARGAME.

4. **COMPARISON OF COURSES OF ACTION.**

5. **DECISION.**

---

a. The restated mission (Step F of mission analysis) goes directly into paragraph 2 of the brigade OPORD after approved by the commander (S3 responsibility).

b. Brigade COA development/analysis and wargaming are accomplished after mission analysis. Course of action development and wargaming result in the production of the OPORD and the CHS annex. During wargaming, the evacuation and treatment facets of the medical plan are synchronized with the maneuver plan. Also, during wargaming, the questions of how many casualties; at what point in the fight (when); where they will occur; and how they are produced (direct fire, artillery, chemical, and so forth) can be forecasted based on input from the S1. This information allows the CHS planner options to select preplanned locations. It also provides the triggers that will allow medical elements to occupy these positions at appropriate times and in a manner that reduces the risk from threat actions. This information becomes the CHS plan and is published in the brigade order. The following is an example of key areas that will be analyzed during this process; they include—

- Casualty estimates broken down to the lowest level possible, by task force, by phase line, and so forth.

- Task organizations established (attachment/detachment or OPCON relationships in division order). Do they adequately support the brigade mission? If not, recommend changes to the brigade commander.

- Division-directed actions as part of the division CHS plan.

- Current CHS unit status (maintenance status on all brigade key items of equipment, both medical and nonmedical, and recommendations of the BSS).

c. Once the task force or maneuver battalions receive the brigade WARNO, they conduct mission analysis and determine their tactical plan. Part of determining their plan is the emplacement of medical treatment elements (BAS or treatment teams). This information is provided to the medical plan/operations officer in the BSS, so he can review the plans from the brigade-level perspective. Time permitting, the BSS plan/operations officer, the FSMC commander, and the HSSO should meet with the medical platoon leaders to synchronize the brigade plan prior to the brigade combined arms rehearsal. Provided below in Table 3-2 is an example of an OPORD format. When the commander approves the OPLAN, it becomes the OPORD. The BSS staff is responsible to the brigade commander for staff supervision of CHS within the brigade. The BSS is also responsible for coordinating DS relationships of organic medical units and medical elements OPCON or attached to the brigade. The brigade commander is updated as required on the status of CHS in the brigade. The brigade OPLAN and OPORD are developed by the S3 section using input from each of the staff elements of the brigade headquarters. The brigade CHS plan is revised or updated based on mission analysis or changes in CHS requirements.

d. The BSS has a primary responsibility for the coordination of corps medical assets in support of the brigade, both OPCON and attached, and for supporting corps MEDEVAC assets positioned forward in the brigade AO. Brigade and corps evacuation assets should be task-organized to support the area of greatest casualty density. All supporting medical elements should be issued the maximum allowable levels of Class VIII and other required supplies. The BSS must establish and maintain continuous communications with the HSSO, the FSMC commander, and the DSS. The medical plan/operations cell maintains a situational map and should use charts to monitor functional areas that will include—

- Units in contact or in high-risk environments.

- Threat situation.

Table 3-2. Operation Order or Plan Outline Format

REFERENCES:
TIME ZONE USED THROUGHOUT THE PLAN (ORDER):
TASK ORGANIZATION:
1. **SITUATION.**
   A. ENEMY FORCE
   B. FRIENDLY FORCE
   C. ATTACHMENT AND DETACHMENTS
   D. ASSUMPTION (OPLAN ONLY)
2. **MISSION.**
3. **EXECUTION.**
   INTENT:
   A. CONCEPT OF OPERATION
      (1) MANEUVERS
      (2) FIRES
      (3) RECONNAISSANCE AND SURVEILLANCE
      (4) INTELLIGENCE
      (5) ENGINEER
      (6) AIR DEFENSE
      (7) INFORMATION OPERATIONS
   B. TASK TO MANEUVER UNITS
      (1) ENGINEER
      (2) AIR DEFENSE
      (3) FIELD ARTILLERY
   C. TASKS TO COMBAT SUPPORT UNITS
      (1) INTELLIGENCE
      (2) FIRE SUPPORT
      (3) SIGNAL
      (4) NBC
      (5) PROVOST MARSHAL
      (6) PSYCHOLOGICAL OPERATIONS
      (7) CIVIL MILITARY
      (8) AS REQUIRED
   D. COORDINATING INSTRUCTIONS
      (1) TIME OR CONDITION WHEN A PLAN OR ORDER BECOMES EFFECTIVE
      (2) COMMANDER'S CRITICAL INFORMATION
      (3) RISK REDUCTION CONTROL MEASURES
      (4) RULES OF ENGAGEMENT
      (5) ENVIRONMENTAL CONSIDERATIONS
      (6) FORCE PROTECTION, AS REQUIRED
      (7) AS REQUIRED
4. **SERVICE SUPPORT.**
   A. SUPPORT CONCEPT
   B. MATERIEL AND SERVICE
   C. MEDICAL EVACUATION AND HOSPITALIZATION
   D. PERSONNEL
   E. CIVIL MILITARY, AS REQUIRED
   F. AS REQUIRED
5. **COMMAND AND SIGNAL.**
   A. COMMAND
   B. SIGNAL

ACKNOWLEDGE:
NAME (COMMANDER'S LAST NAME)
RANK (COMMANDER'S RANK)
OFFICIAL: NAME AND POSITION
ANNEXES:

(CLASSIFICATION)

SEE FM 101 5 FOR DEFINITIVE INFORMATION ON OPERATION PLANS/ORDERS.

- Evacuation routes and/or main supply route status.

- Supporting corps ground and air ambulance assets.

- Army airspace command and control overlays.

- Status of evacuation platforms (all assets under the brigade's control).

- Supply status, to include critical Class VIII shortages.

- Pending resupply missions from corps.

- Critical medical personnel and equipment shortages.

- Medical maintenance backlog.

- Patient status board (for example, awaiting evacuation).

- Blood status.

- Dirty routes/patient decontamination sites.

- Location of BAS (current/projected).

- Area medical support responsibilities.

3-5.   Rehearsal

Developing a good brigade CHS plan is not an easy process. It requires a major coordinated effort with sound preparation, discipline, and significant amounts of the precious commodity—leader time. Properly rehearsing the plan is a critical step in achieving synchronized execution with the brigade commander's plan. The brigade rehearsal provides an excellent opportunity to practice C2 and integrate the CHS operations. For successful implementation of the CHS annex of the brigade plan, the CHS plan must be coordinated and synchronized with the maneuver plan so that CHS requirements are met. The BSS provides coordinating instruction to the brigade medical elements as the plan is developed. This permits informed development and affords the time to better develop the initial plans. To achieve optimal synchronization, the CHS plan is rehearsed as an integral part of the combined arms plan at the combined arms rehearsal. The CHS rehearsal by itself as a technique will increase understanding and synchronization, but is not as effective as when it is integrated into the combined arms rehearsal. The rehearsal of the CHS plan will allow subordinate medical elements and leaders to analyze the tactical CHS plan to ascertain its feasibility, its common sense, and the adequacy of its C2 measures prior to execution.

   a.   Medical platoon leaders of the maneuver battalions also provide input to the task force CHS plan. In the digitized brigade, the BSS develops the concept for the CHS plan. During the decision-making/

orders process, the CHS planners identify critical events and synchronize their plans. In addition to medical locations on the CSS overlay, these plans indicate the triggers for CHS events. At the brigade rehearsal, the brigade leaders practice their synchronized plans that include CHS. The sequence of events for the CHS portion of the brigade rehearsal includes—

• The FSMC commander and ambulance platoon leader practicing execution of triggers for AXP movement.

• The FSMC commanders detailing the concept and procedures for MEDEVAC (both ground and air ambulances) in the brigade.

• The battalion/task force executive officer (XO) or S4 explains triggers for BAS and combat trains command post (CTCP) movement and ensures that brigade level and adjacent units understand their internal plan.

The BCT medical elements with area support missions indicate which units are supported and the areas they cover. They will also provide projected triggers and times they will be at projected locations.

    b.   The CSS/CHS annex of the brigade OPORD that includes map overlays is the culmination of the medical planning efforts and the CHS rehearsal is the culmination of the preparation phase for an operation. In the digitized division, the brigade medical planner has the responsibility for rehearsing CHS operations. Rehearsals are done to achieve a common understanding and a picture of how the plan will be implemented.

• All plans must be complete prior to the CHS rehearsal.

• The brigade OPORD is then issued through effective troop leading procedures.

• The CHS rehearsals should focus on the events that are critical to mission accomplishment. A successful rehearsal ensures explicit understanding by subordinate medical leaders of their individual missions, how their missions relate to each other, and how each mission relates to the maneuver commander's plan. It is important for all medical echelons to see the total CHS concept.

• Rehearsing key CHS actions allows participants to become familiar with the operation and to visualize the "triggers" which identify the circumstances and timing for friendly actions. This visual impression helps them understand both their environment and their relationship to other units during the operation. The repetition of critical medical tasks during the rehearsal helps leaders remember the sequence of key actions within the operation and when they are executed.

NOTE

To achieve the last two bullets above, the CHS rehearsal needs to be a part of the Brigade combined arms rehearsal along with all the battlefield operating systems. It is just as important for the supported units to understand the CHS plan as it is for the medical unit to understand the maneuver plan.

c. Planning and rehearsing CSS is the responsibility of the brigade S4. His responsibilities include—

- Deciding what events must be rehearsed in coordination with the medical planner and/or brigade surgeon.

- Determining all the CHS activities on the CSS synchronization matrix to be rehearsed.

- Focusing on key events that must be carried out from just prior to line of departure (LD) time, through reorganization and consolidation.

- Deciding on the participants and observers for the rehearsal.

- Participants providing information or performing actions that cause triggered events to occur. Observers do not have a direct impact on triggered events, but gather information and answer questions as required.

- The FSB support operations officer representing CSS elements of the FSB along with FSB company commanders. The CHS activities may include the brigade surgeon, the brigade medical planner, the FSB HSSO, and the FSMC commander, his ambulance and treatment platoon leaders, and the forward support MEDEVAC team (FSMT).

NOTE

As many executors of the plan as possible should be included in the rehearsal. The FSMC commander and the ambulance platoon leader as a minimum are participants for the FSB. The task force medical platoon leaders should also be active participants.

- All task force medical platoon leaders participating. The reserve task force will rehearse the conditions under which the commander expects to employ them; this medical platoon leader should participate as well. If the medical platoon leader cannot participate, the medical platoon sergeant should represent that task force.

- Allow adequate time between the end of planning and the beginning of the CHS rehearsal for subordinates to develop their plans and synchronize them with the brigade (this is normally accomplished using the $1/3 - 2/3$ rule).

- Holding the CHS rehearsal on the same terrain model as the combined arms rehearsal. (Ideally it should be part of the combined arms rehearsal.)

The BSS must inform all CHS personnel about the CHS rehearsal. This may be SOP or issued as part of the CHS annex in the brigade order. If not, then send a fragmentary order to all medical elements with time, place, and required participants.

Section II. CONDUCTING COMBAT HEALTH SUPPORT FOR MILITARY ACTIONS

3-6. Force Projection

a. The force projection process includes eight related activities. These activities include—mobilization; predeployment; deployment (including basing); entry (including reception, staging, onward movement, and integration) and force buildup; decisive operations; postconflict and postcrisis actions; redeployment; and demobilization. For detailed information on the force projection process, see FMs 100-7 and 100-17.

b. The first rule of anticipation for the staff of the BSS in a force projection era is to expect to be alerted and deployed. A high level of anticipation causes military forces to mentally and physically prepare for force projection. If the brigade has been assigned a region of focus in peacetime, planning can occur long before alert and deployment. Appropriate actions include ordering and posting maps, studying available infrastructures, familiarizing soldiers with language, training soldiers for deployment, and sensitizing soldiers to a particular culture. Key to successful anticipation is continuous force tracking, total asset visibility during deployment, and continuous intelligence preparation of the battlefield (IPB) of the contingency area.

c. Many of the missions assigned to US Army forces will be received as short-notice deployments (such as deployments in support of contingency operations). The advance preparation time will be limited. Normally, due to the sensitivity of the operations security (OPSEC) level of the operation, the number of individuals that engaged in the planning process could be restricted. It is, therefore, necessary that the BSS ensure that the medical platoons organic to the brigade's maneuver battalion are administratively ready for short-notice deployment. For definitive information on the CHS aspects of short-notice deployments for stability operations and support operations, see FMs 8-42 and 100-5.

3-7. Combat Health Support for the Offense and the Defense

a. Support to the Offense.

(1) The offense is the decisive form of war, the commander's only means of attaining a positive goal, or of completely destroying an enemy force (FM 100-5). Rapid movement, deep penetrations, aggressive action, and the ability to sustain momentum regardless of counterfires and countermeasures characterize the offense.

(2) When developing the CHS plan to support the offense, the CHS planner must consider many factors (FM 8-55). The forms of maneuver, as well as the threat's capabilities, influence the character of the patient workload and its time and space distribution. The analysis of this workload determines the allocation of CHS resources and the location or relocation of MTFs.

(3) Combat health support for offensive operations must be responsive to several essential characteristics. As operations achieve success, the areas of casualty density move away from the supporting MTF. This causes the routes of MEDEVAC to lengthen. Heaviest patient workloads occur during disruption of the threat's main defenses, at terrain or tactical barriers, during the assault on final objectives, and during threat counterattacks. The accurate prediction of these workload points by the CHS planner is essential if MEDEVAC operations are to be successful.

(4) As advancing combat formations extend control of the battle area, supporting medical elements have the opportunity to clear the battlefield. This facilitates the acquisition of the battle wounded and reduces the vital time elapsed between wounding and treatment. There are two basic problems confronting the supporting medical units and MEDEVAC elements. First, contact with the supported units must be maintained. Responsibility for the contact follows the normal CHS pattern—higher echelon evacuates from lower echelon. Contact is maintained by forward deployed air and ground evacuation resources. Secondly, the mobility of the MTFs supporting the combat formations must be maintained. The requirement for prompt MEDEVAC of patients from forward MTFs requires available ambulances to be echeloned well forward from the outset. Air ambulance and ground ambulance support beyond the capabilities of the FSMC is requested from the supporting corps MEDEVAC battalion. The requirement for periodic movement of large numbers of patients from divisional and corps facilities further stresses the MEDEVAC system.

(5) In traditional combat operations, the major casualty area of the operation is normally the zone of the main attack. As the main attack accomplishes the primary task of the tactical combat force, it receives first priority in the allocation of combat power. The allocation of combat forces dictates roughly the areas that are likely to have the greatest casualty density. In the division, CHS (Echelon I) for the brigade is provided by the maneuver battalion medical platoons. Each platoon consists of three treatment teams, an ambulance section, and a combat medic's section. The medical platoon operates the BAS, places combat medics in DS of the maneuver companies, provides patient evacuation from forward areas, and deploys treatment teams in DS of the maneuver battalion elements for up to 48 hours without resupply. The FSMC (Echelon II) located in the BSA provides MEDEVAC support from the BAS back to the BSA and reinforces treatment capabilities at BASs for limited periods of time. When combat operations commence, the medical platoon normally locates its BAS as far forward as combat operations permit. As the battle moves from the original area of contact, coordinated movement of the three treatment teams are able to provide continuous CHS. Once patients are received, a treatment team from the BAS will care for and treat these patients until their MEDEVAC or appropriate disposition. The remaining teams of the BAS move with the battle and provide CHS to the maneuver elements according to the task force order or current execution conditions. If patients are received, one of the other treatment teams performs its treatment and evacuation mission. After MEDEVAC or appropriate disposition of their patients, the treatment team prepares for its next move. This "leap frog" technique provides for maximum utilization of medical platoon treatment teams and permits continuous uninterrupted CHS to maneuver battalions on the move. Each of the above actions must be coordinated with the CTCP and the supporting FSMC.

(6) In operations that feature deep battles with weapons of mass destruction targeted at supporting logistical bases, mass casualty operations could be conducted in rear areas.

(7)   Types of operations in the offense include—

(a)   *Movement to contact.* Medical evacuation support in movement to contact is keyed to the tactical plan. Prior deployment of FSMC ground ambulances with the maneuver battalion's organic medical platoons permits uninterrupted and effective MEDEVAC support from the BAS to the FSMC located in the BSA. Movement to contact operations are executed when there is little or no threat information. The FSMC and treatment teams from maneuver BAS in support of these operations must maintain their flexibility and be prepared to adjust CHS support once contact is established.

(b)   *Exploitation and pursuit.* Medical evacuation support of exploitation and pursuit operations resemble those discussed for the envelopment (paragraph 3-8a[2]). Since exploitation and pursuit operations can rarely be planned in detail, evacuation operations must adhere to TSOPs and innovative C2. These actions are often characterized by—

- Fewer casualties.

- Decentralized operations.

- Unsecured ground evacuation routes.

- Exceptionally long distances for evacuation.

- Increased reliance on convoys and air ambulances.

- More difficult communications (maximum radio range).

(c)   *Deliberate attack.* The deliberate attack is based on a more detailed knowledge of the threat disposition and likely actions. The brigade's actions in contact will be more predictable than the fluid situation found in the movement to contact, or exploitation and pursuit. Specific terrain and routes/ avenues of approach can be selected. Units can conduct at least a map reconnaissance of their planned locations. While there may be CHS requirements during the approach, the assault on the objective will produce the greatest number of casualties. Some of the CHS considerations for the deliberate attack include—

- Higher percentage of casualties.

- Casualties will be more concentrated in time and space.

- Treatment teams moving to the objective instead of evacuating patients from the objective to the treatment teams once the objective is secured.

- Use of air ambulance to overcome some obstacles may be required.

b.   *Support to the Defense.* There are three forms of the defense: area defense, mobile defense, and retrograde. The area defense concentrates on denying threat access to designated terrain for a specific period of time, rather than on the outright destruction of the threat. The mobile defense focuses on denying the threat force by allowing him to advance to a point where he is exposed to a decisive counterattack by the striking force. The primary defeat mechanism, the counterattack, is supplemented by the fires of the fixing force. The third form of defense is the retrograde. The retrograde is an organized movement to the rear and away from the threat. The threat could force these operations or a commander can execute them voluntarily. Delay, withdrawal, and retirement are the three forms of retrograde operation.

(1) Combat health support is generally more difficult to provide in the defense. The patient load reflects lower casualty rates, but threat actions and the maneuver of combat forces complicate forward area patient acquisition. Medical personnel are permitted much less time to reach the patient, complete vital EMT, and remove him from the battle site. Increased casualties among exposed medical personnel further reduce the medical treatment and evacuation capabilities. Heaviest patient workloads, including those produced by threat artillery and NBC weapons, can be expected during the preparation or initial phase of the threat attack and in the counterattack phase. The threat attack can disrupt ground and air routes and delay evacuation of patients to and from treatment elements. The depth and dispersion of the defense create significant time and distance problems for evacuation assets. Combat elements could be forced to withdraw while carrying their remaining patients to the rear. The threat exercises the initiative early in the operation, which could preclude accurate prediction of initial areas of casualty density. This makes the effective integration of air assets into the MEDEVAC plan essential. The use of air ambulances must be coordinated with the FSMT, normally positioned in the BSA. The utilization of corps air ambulances must be integrated into the CHS annex to the OPORD and also into the brigade's A2C2 annex. In addition, frequent coordination with the corps MEDEVAC team is essential.

(2) The CHS requirements for retrograde operations can vary widely depending upon the tactical plan, the threat reaction, and the METT-TC factors. Firm rules that apply equally to all types of retrograde operations are not feasible, but considerations include—

- A requirement for maximum security and secrecy in movement.

- The influence of refugee movement conducted in friendly territory, which could impede MEDEVAC missions.

- The integration of evacuation routes and obstacle plans.

- Difficulties in controlling and coordinating movements of the force, that could produce lucrative targets for the threat.

- Movements at night or during periods of limited visibility.

- Time and means available to remove patients from the battlefield. In stable situations and in the advance, time is important only as it affects the physical well-being of the wounded. In retrograde operations, time is more important. As available time decreases, CHS managers at all echelons closely evaluate the capability to collect, treat, and evacuate all patients.

- Medical evacuation routes required for the movement of troops and materiel. This causes patient evacuation in retrograde movements to be more difficult than in any other type of operation.

The threat could disrupt C2 and communications. Successful MEDEVAC requires including ambulances on the priority list for movement; providing for the transportation of the slightly wounded in cargo vehicles; and providing guidance to subordinate commanders defining their responsibilities in collecting and evacuating patients. Special emphasis must be placed on the triage of patients and consideration given to the type of transportation assets available for evacuation.

• Decisions concerning patients left behind. When the patient load exceeds the means to move them, the tactical commander must make the decision as to whether patients are to be left behind. The medical staff officer keeps the tactical commander informed so that he can make timely decisions. Medical personnel and supplies must be left with patients who cannot be evacuated. (Refer to FM 8-10 for additional information.)

3-8. Combat Health Support for Maneuver and Enabling Operations

a. Choices of Maneuver.

(1) *Penetration.* In this tactic, the attack passes through the threat's principal defensive position, ruptures it, and neutralizes or destroys the threat forces. Of all forms of offensive maneuver, the penetration of main threat defenses normally produces the heaviest patient workload. Patient acquisition starts slowly, but becomes more rapid as the attack progresses. The evacuation routes lengthen as the operation progresses. Heavy preparatory fires which can evoke heavy return fire often precede the penetration maneuver. These threat fires could modify the decision to place evacuation assets as far forward as possible. The FSMC can reinforce the penetration force medical elements. Patient evacuation could be slow and difficult due to bottleneck at the penetration. Medical evacuation support problems multiply when some combat units remain near the point of original penetration. This is done to hold or widen the gap in threat defenses while the bulk of tactical combat forces exploit or pursue the threat. Treatment elements are placed near each shoulder of the penetration; ground evacuation cannot take place across an avenue of heavy combat traffic. Because of the heavy traffic, the area of the penetration is normally a target for both conventional and NBC weapons. The trigger to push treatment team/BASs through the penetration and where they will go must be identified in the OPORD.

(2) *Envelopment.* In the envelopment, the main or enveloping attack passes around or over the threat's principal defensive positions. The purpose is to seize objectives that cut the threat's escape routes and subject him to destruction in place from flank to rear. Since the envelopment maneuver involves no direct breach of the threat's principal defensive positions, the MEDEVAC system is not confronted with a heavy workload in the opening phase. However, ambulances are positioned well forward in all echelons of CHS to quickly evacuate the patients generated by suddenly occurring contact. Medical treatment facilities moving with their respective formations assist with clearing the battlefield to reduce delays in treatment. After triage and treatment, the patients are evacuated to MTFs in the rear by supporting ground ambulances from the FSMC. When the isolated nature of the envelopment maneuver precludes prompt evacuation, the patients are carried forward with the treatment element. This must be planned for in detail and is an extreme measure when no other option is feasible. Expect an increase in mortality from wounds. Again, nonmedical vehicles could be pressed into emergency use for this purpose. When patients must be carried forward with the enveloping forces, CHS commanders use halts at assembly areas and phase lines to

arrange combat protection for ground ambulance convoys through unsecured areas. Further, the commander should take advantage of friendly fires and suppression of threat air defenses to call for prearranged air ambulance support missions, or emergency use of medium-lift helicopter backhaul capabilities.

(3) *Infiltration.*

(*a*) Infiltration is a choice of maneuver used during offensive operations. The division can attack after infiltration or use it as a means of obtaining intelligence and harassing the threat. Though it is not restricted to small units or dismounted actions, the division employs these techniques with a portion of its units, in conjunction with offensive operations conducted by the remainder of its units.

(*b*) Combat health support of infiltration is restricted by the amount of medical equipment, supplies, and transportation assets that can be introduced into the attack area. No deployment of BAS treatment teams without their organic transportation should be attempted. Elements of unit-level CHS should be accompanied by their organic vehicles, and ambulances should receive priority for deployment. It could be necessary to man-carry enough BAS equipment into the attack area to provide EMT and ATM; this, however, results in degrading mobility. When the element is committed without its ambulances, patients are evacuated to the BAS by litter bearer teams. These litter teams must be designated and equipped by the commanders in their orders. Noise, light, and litter discipline during evacuation in an infiltration depends on how the casualty was wounded. Disease and nonbattle-injured soldiers may not have been noticed by the enemy. If the casualty is a battle injury, the enemy has already detected that element. Once the enemy has detected and engaged the force, causing casualties, maximum allowable use of standard and nonstandard MEDEVAC platforms should be used. This will increase lift capabilities and save time and soldier's lives. Patient evacuation from the BAS and medical resupply of the force could be provided by litter bearers, depending upon distances and degree of secrecy required.

(*c*) When airborne and air assault forces are used, infiltrating elements can land at various points within the threat's rear area and proceed on foot to designated attack positions. As in surface movement, the amount of medical equipment taken could be limited. In airborne operations, the evacuation of patients will be by litter bearers or frontline ambulances to collecting points or the BAS and then by FSMC ambulances to the clearing station operated by the FSMC treatment platoon. In air assault operations, the evacuation is by litter bearers to collecting points or the BAS and then by air ambulances to a clearing station. Once the combat element begins the assault on the objective, secrecy is no longer important and its isolated location requires CHS characteristic to airborne and air assault operations until ground linkup.

(4) *Turning movement.* A turning movement is a variation of the envelopment in which the attacking force passes around or over the threat's principal defense positions to secure objectives deep in the threat's rear and force the threat to abandon his position, or to divert major forces to meet the threat. As stated above, the turning movement is a variant to the envelopment in which the attacker attempts to avoid the defense entirely; rather, the attacker seeks to secure key terrain deep in the threat's rear and along his lines of communication (LOC). Faced with a major threat to his rear, the threat is thus "turned" out of his defensive positions and forced to attack rearward at a disadvantage. Medical evacuation support to the turning movement is provided basically in the same manner as to the envelopment. As the operation is conducted in the threat's rear area, LOC and evacuation routes could be unsecured, resulting in delays in resupply and evacuation.

b. *Enabling Operations.*

(1) *Passage of lines.* This situation presents a challenge for the CHS planner. There will be a number of MEDEVAC units using the same air and road networks. Coordination and synchronization are essential if confusion and overevacuation are to be avoided. The medical units of the force manning the line should provide area support to the force passing through. This allows continued mobility for the moving force. The below information facilitates this coordination.

- Radio frequencies and call signs.

- Operation plans and TSOPs.

- Location of MTFs.

- Location of patient collecting points and AXPs.

- Main supply route, forward arming and refueling points, and A2C2 data.

(2) *Security operations.* Security operations obtain information about the enemy and provide reaction time, maneuver space, and protection to the main body. Security operations are characterized by aggressive reconnaissance to reduce terrain and enemy unknowns, gaining and maintaining contact with the enemy to ensure continuous information and provide early and accurate reporting of information to the protected force. See FM 17-95 for definitive information on security operations. The discussion below focuses on how CHS is provided for security operations. Security operations include the following missions:

- Cover.

- Screen.

- Guard.

- Area security.

(a) *Cover.* The covering forces are dependent upon organic resources found in the maneuver battalion medical platoon for initial support. The level of command for the covering force determines the responsibility for the subsequent evacuation plan. In a corps covering force, for example, the corps CHS structure has the responsibility for establishing and operating the MEDEVAC system to support the forward deployed corps forces. This is done to prevent the tactical combat force following the covering forces from becoming overloaded with patients prior to the hand off and passage of lines. The use of patient collecting points, AXPs, and nonmedical transportation assets (casualty evacuation) to move the wounded is essential. The covering force battle could be extremely violent. Patient loads will be high and the distance to MTFs can be much longer than usual. The effectiveness of the MEDEVAC system depends upon the forward positioning of a number of ground ambulances and the effective integration of corps air ambulances into the evacuation plan.

(b) *Screen.* The primary purpose of a screen is to provide early warning to the main body. Screen missions are defensive in nature and largely accomplished by establishing a series of observation posts and conducting patrols to ensure adequate surveillance of the assigned sector. The screen provides the protected force with the least protection of any security mission. Combat health support will be provided by organic medical elements and ambulances teams deployed from the supporting medical company.

(c) *Advance, flank, and rear guards.* A guard force accomplishes all the task of a screening force. Additionally, a guard force prevents enemy ground observation of and direct fire against the main body. A guard force reconnoiters, attacks, defends, and delays as necessary to accomplish its mission. A guard force normally operates within the range of the main body's indirect fire weapons. A guard force is deployed over a narrower front, then a screen to permit concentration of combat power. These forces normally receive MEDEVAC support through the attachment of evacuation teams. The teams evacuate patients to predesignated patient collecting points along a main axis of advance or to the nearest treatment element providing area support. Employment of air ambulances provide a measure of agility and flexibility.

(d) *Area security.* Area security is a form of security that includes reconnaissance and security by designated personnel of airfields, unit convoys, facilities, main supply routes, LOCs, equipment, and critical points. Area security operations are conducted to deny the enemy the ability to influence actions in a specific area or to deny the enemy use of an area for his own purpose. This may entail occupying and establishing a 360-degree perimeter around the area being secured, or taking actions to destroy enemy forces already present. The area to be secured may range from specific points (bridges, defiles) to areas such as terrain features (ridgelines, hills) to large population centers and adjacent areas. Combat health support will be provided by organic and attached medical elements. In area security, Echelon I CHS is provided by organic or attached treatment teams. Echelon II CHS is provided by the supporting medical company via DS and on an area support basis. Depending on the type of area security operations being conducted, both air and ground ambulances may be employed.

(3) *River crossing operations.* The river barrier itself exerts decisive influence on the use of medical units. An attack across a river line creates a CHS delivery problem comparable to that of the amphibious assault. Combat health support elements cross as soon as combat operations permit. Early crossing of treatment elements reduces turnaround time for all crossing equipment that is used to load patients on the far shore. Maximum use of air ambulance assets is made to prevent excessive patient buildup in far shore treatment facilities. Near-shore MTFs are placed as far forward as assault operations and protective considerations permit to reduce ambulance shuttle distances from off-loading points. For detailed information on river-crossing operations, refer to FM 90-13. Rescuing casualties in the water must be considered by the task force medical planner.

(4) *Reconnaissance operations.* The reconnaissance in force is an attack to discover and test the threat's position and strength or to develop other intelligence. The tactical combat force usually probes with multiple combat units of limited size, retaining sufficient reserves to quickly exploit known threat weaknesses. Combat health support techniques follow those discussed above for a movement to contact. Ambulances are positioned well forward and moved at night to enhance secrecy. The echeloning of ambulances is an indication to the threat that an attack is imminent due to the forward placement of CHS.

Clearing stations are not established until a significant patient workload develops. Patients received at BAS of reconnoitering units are evacuated to clearing stations as early as practical, or are carried forward with the force until a suitable opportunity for evacuation presents itself. The maximum possible use of air ambulance assets is made to cover extended distances and to overcome potentially unsecured ground evacuation routes.

(5) *Unified action.* The majority of the operations occurring at the present time are joint, interagency, or multinational operations. The CHS planner must determine in the initial planning stages of these operations whose responsibility it is to provide MEDEVAC support to the force. The CHS planner must also ensure that duplications in support do not exist, that guidelines are established as to eligible beneficiaries, when individuals are to be returned to their own nation's health care delivery system, and what mechanisms exist for reimbursement of services. For additional information, refer to FM 8-42 and JP 4-02.

(6) *Integrated warfare operations.* Medical evacuation in an NBC environment is discussed in FMs 8-10-4, 8-10-6, and 8-10-7.

3-9. Combat Health Support During Night Operations

The BSS must anticipate that the brigade does a substantial amount of its work at night or in limited visibility. For night operations to be successful, they require tactics, techniques, and procedures that maximize the night-fighting technological advantages. Command and control is one of the most important factors in conducting night operations. The mission of maneuver forces is to destroy the enemy without committing fratricide. To achieve this end state, all soldiers must operate as efficiently at night as during the day. Moreover, leaders must master night C2.

a. *General Considerations.*

(1) The DSS and BSS, along with medical company commanders, must anticipate that supported maneuver brigades and division units do a substantial amount of their work at night or in limited visibility. They must ensure that TSOPs are available and used throughout the division and brigade for providing MEDEVAC and treatment at night. Real-life trauma care at night will be enhanced by the ability to use white light (visible light) at the earliest opportunity. Therefore, medical units/elements must establish standard procedures to use white light without compromising the tactical environment. This means training to erect shelters as soon as possible and routinely during hours of darkness. Personnel must understand that some shelters block visible light but those same shelters glow when viewed through night vision goggles (NVGs). In some extremely mobile situation ambulance/vehicles could be used to enclose patients and care providers thus allowing treatment to proceed under white-light conditions. The DSS and BSS, along with medical company commanders, must understand the technology and their capabilities for conducting night operations. The brigade surgeons and medical company commanders should know how to use both far infrared devices (and how their capabilities can enhance CHS operations at night) such as the combat identification panel (CIP) and near infrared devices such as the BUD light and Phoenix light. See the discussion below on infrared and night vision devices. They need to know status and amount of equipment on-hand and to identify equipment needed. The BSS must plan the SOPs and METT-TC specific techniques

necessary to perform the CHS mission. For these types of operations, the commander should be advised to consider—

- Appropriating civilian buildings to reduce light and thermal signatures.

- Lightproofing shelters.

- Using nonvisible spectrum light in conjunction with night vision devices.

- Reducing noise signature to a minimum.

(2)   In addition, divisional units, the DSA, and BSAs are susceptible to a night attack. This further slows logistics and CHS activities. Use of chemical lights may be applicable. However, overuse of chemical lights degrades light discipline and security. Chemical lights are visible from a distance of a kilometer or more. Possible techniques for medical units/elements to use include—

- Chemical lights to light CP areas, thus eliminating generator noise and thermal signature.

- Magnetic holders to allow placement of color chemical lights on vehicles.

- Chemical lights to illuminate vehicle engine compartment areas for night repairs.

- Chemical light holders to regulate the amount and direction of light.

   b.   *Combat Health Support Considerations.*

(1)   Light discipline requirements affect CHS operations much as they do supply and maintenance operations. Medical units/elements will use additional fuel to operate power generation equipment. Treatment operations require lightproof shelters. Patient acquisition is more difficult. Units should employ some sort of casualty-marking system such as luminous tape.

(2)   Limited visibility slows MEDEVAC. This requires additional ground ambulances to compensate. In the offense, ambulances move forward with BASs. However, personnel have to accomplish this movement carefully to avoid signaling the threat. Personnel use predesignated AXPs. Medical evacuation by air ambulance is difficult and requires precise grid coordinates as well as prearranged signals and frequencies. As in daylight, CHS operations conducted at night require active participation of all involved units. Operational procedures must include near and far recognition, signaling, predetermined marking of patient collection points, routes, and MTFs. Maximum use of modern navigation tools such as the Global Positioning System (GPS), infrared, and night visions devices will enhance the ability of medical units/personnel to carry out CHS in support of night missions. Night operating procedures must be routine and practiced as a part of routine operating procedures. This is especially true for medical units/personnel since they have a 24-hour responsibility under all conditions, not just combat operations.

   c.   *Infrared and Night Vision Devices.*

(1)   Far-infrared device, such as the CIP, is a QUICK FIX device for friendly identification. The thermal taped-covered CIP provides an aid in distinguishing friendly from threat vehicles when thermal sights are used.   Combat identification panels do not replace current acquisition, identification, or engagement procedures.   They provide a device visible through thermal sights to increase situational awareness and provide a safety net at normal engagement range. For additional information on the CIP go to http://call.army.mil/call/user-gui/95-3/chapter2.htm.   These devices can be used to further identify medical vehicle and units.

(2)   Near-infrared devices that aid in C2 may be used for signaling and marking devices. The infrared beam is an effective means to increase situational awareness, improve identification, and increase combat effectiveness.   These devices reduce fratricide risk when used for marking obstacles, seized terrain, and breached sites. Additionally, these lights are super signaling devices (that is, configuring of certain patterns to indicate unit identification, turning on/off to signal accomplishment of a task, crossing a phase line, signaling from one ground position to another specific position, or from ground to air). They are also useful in specialized units such as pathfinders for marking pickup, drop, or landing zones (LZs). These are excellent devices for near recognition signaling to guide incoming evacuation vehicles.

(a)   *BUD light*. The BUD light operates using active near-infrared light viewed through image-intensifying devices. These image-intensifying devices are only effective during nighttime conditions. Near-infrared devices can be directional or omnidirectional and emit a steady pulse or a codable pulse. The BUD light is a compact near-infrared source using a standard 9-volt (BA-3090) battery as its power source. Both the BUD light and its power source will fit in the palm of the hand. The average life span of the battery power for a BUD light is 8 hours of continuous use. The near infrared pulse emitted by the BUD light is similar to a strobe light, and pulses every 2 seconds. It is invisible to the naked eye and thermal imagers. The pulse is clearly visible out to 4 kilometers under optimal conditions when pointing the beam directly at the viewer. The directional characteristic of the beam makes it possible to limit observation by an enemy. If used to mark vehicles, care should be taken to minimize the light illuminating the vehicle's surface. The enemy has to have image intensifying devices to see the lights directly; however, they may see the light being reflected off of vehicles when the lights are employed in a directional mode. This device is most effective for C2 purposes. The BUD light is also very useful for dismounted operations at night.

(b)   *Phoenix light*. The Phoenix light operates using active near-infrared light viewed through image intensifying devices. The Phoenix light can be used as a codable infrared beacon. The light is powered by a standard 9-volt (BA-3090) battery. The Phoenix light is ideal for use when positive identification at night must be made out to 4 kilometers under optimal conditions. The infrared beacon has a range equal to the BUD light. One advantage is the ability to code many beacons with different codes (sequence of flashes—including Morse code—up to 4 seconds) enabling anyone to be distinguished in a group. A programmed sequence will repeat until canceled or when the battery expires (same as BUD light). Operating instructions include connecting the battery to the Phoenix light. Using a metal object—a coin is best—make connection across the two pins on top of the light. A microminiature red indicator flashes the sequence as the code is entered. At the end of the 4-second memory, a green microminiature indicator will flash, indicating the end of the input sequence. The Phoenix light is now emitting the desired code. To check the code, make a connection across the pins. The green microminiature indicator will flash the code. To change the code, disconnect the battery and repeat the instructions. The Phoenix light also can be used during dismounted operations. The programming of a code can assist in distinguishing one unit from another. An active Phoenix light or BUD light can be covered or uncovered as necessary to ensure the light is visible only when necessary.

        (*c*) *Night vision devices.* There are numerous types of night vision devices in the Army inventory but this subparagraph will focus on what the FSMC has on its TOE. Each vehicle in the FSMC will have two night vision devices. The wheeled vehicle driver will use either the AN/PVS-7B (discussed below) or the driver's vision enhancer (DVE). The DVE is a thermal imaging system capable of operating in degraded visibility conditions such as fog, dust, smoke, and darkness. In conditions of reduced visibility, the DVE allows a vehicle to maintain speeds up to 55 to 60 percent of those attained during normal daylight operations. Unlike traditional night vision devices that magnify ambient light, the DVE generates a picture based on very minute variances in temperature in the surrounding environment. It gives the operator visibility to the horizon in total darkness and the ability to recognize a 22-inch object at a distance of 360 feet. It can elevate 35 degrees, depress 5 degrees, and rotate 170 degrees in either direction. The DVE consists of a sensor module, display control module, positioning module, wiring harness, and mounting equipment. A combat DVE and a tactical wheeled vehicle DVE will be available. The tracked ambulances (M113) and M577 tracked treatment vehicle drivers will use DVE if available, or will continue to wear NVGs. The NVGs (AN/PVS-7B) is a hand-held, head-mounted, or helmet-mounted night vision system that enables walking, driving, weapons firing, short-range surveillance, map reading, treatment of patients, vehicle maintenance in both moonlight and starlight. It has an infrared projector that provides illumination at close ranges and that can be used for signaling. There is a high-light level shutoff if the device is exposed to damaging levels of bright light. There is a compass that attaches to the device that allows for reading an azimuth through the goggles. This device has a weight of 1.5 pounds and operates on two AA batteries. Armored medical vehicles (M577, treatment vehicle, M113, armored ambulance, and the new armored evacuation vehicle [AEV] when fielded) have infrared headlights. These infrared headlights can be used for assisting drivers who wear NVGs and can be used for signaling. As with all lights, extreme caution must be taken in tactical situations. The infrared headlights are typically very bright to personnel wearing NVGs.

    d. *Example Techniques for Using Chemical Lights for Marking and Signaling.*

NOTE

Techniques are only limited to available equipment and imagination.
The METT-TC should always take precedence.

    (1) For marking, chemical lights can be placed inside standard military short or long tent stakes/pickets to mark routes and positions. The concave side of the tent stake contains the chemical light and the convex side faces the most likely direction of enemy observation. This techniques controls the direction of the light while assisting with such things as a MEDEVAC route, supported unit collection point, AXP, or link up point identification.

    (2) For signaling, tying a chemical light to a length of cord or string and slinging it in a circle overhead is an unmistakable signal. This only needs to be use once for recognition (radio) to be established and is ended once the signal is seen. This technique makes use of widely available common supplies. It is especially useful for a unit guiding an incoming ground or air ambulance.

3-10. Combat Health Support for Stability Operations

a. *Overview of Stability Operations.*

(1) Stability operations apply military power to influence the political environment, facilitate diplomacy, and interrupt specified illegal activities. Stability operations include both developmental and coercive actions. *Developmental actions* enhance a government's willingness and ability to care for its people. *Coercive actions* apply carefully prescribed limited force and/or the threat of force to achieve objectives. The types of activities conducted in stability operations include—

- Peace operations.

- Operations in support of diplomatic efforts.

- Combatting terrorism operations.

- Counterdrug operations.

- Noncombatant evacuation operations (NEO).

- Arms control.

- Nation assistance and foreign internal defense.

- Support to insurgencies and counterinsurgencies.

- Shows of force.

- Civil disturbance operations.

(2) While each operation in this environment is unique, there are seven broad imperatives that enhance the deployed forces' ability to develop concepts and schemes for executing stability operations. These imperatives are—

- Stressing force protection.

- Emphasizing information operations.

- Maximizing interagency, joint, and multinational cooperation.

- Displaying the capability to apply force without threatening.

- Understanding the potential for disproportionate consequences to individual and small-unit actions.

- Applying force selectively and discriminatingly.

- Acting decisively to prevent escalation.

  b.   Combat Health Support for Stability Operations.

(1)   Combat health support to forces deployed for stability operations is dependent upon the specific type of operation, anticipated duration of the operation, number of forces deployed, theater evacuation policy, medical troop ceiling, and anticipated level of violence. In most situations, CHS follows the traditional support provided to combat forces. If there is a shortened theater evacuation policy, a limited medical troop ceiling, and limited hospitalization assets within the AO, organic and DS ambulance support is provided from the point of injury to the supporting Echelons I or II MTF. The patient is stabilized at the MTF, then evacuated from the treatment element to an airfield for evacuation out of the theater.

(2)   During NEO, those persons who are injured, wounded, or ill are treated and stabilized by the medical element accompanying the NEO force. Once stabilized, the NEO force evacuates them. In NEO conducted in a permissive environment (no apparent physical threat to the evacuees), sick, injured, or wounded persons should be evacuated on dedicated MEDEVAC platforms, if at all possible. In an uncertain or hostile environment, the transportation assets used to insert and extract the NEO force are normally used to evacuate the patients. The medical personnel accompanying the force provide en route medical care until the NEO force reaches an intermediate staging base (ISB) or safe haven. Those evacuees requiring medical care are then transferred to dedicated MEDEVAC platforms for further evacuation to MTFs capable of providing the required care.

(3)   During combatting terrorism operations, planning considerations for CHS include—

- Using medical and nonmedical transportation assets to evacuate casualties in mass casualty situations. If nonmedical assets are used, planning should include augmenting these assets with medical personnel, adequate litters, and medical supplies to provide en route medical care.

- Applying techniques for acquiring and evacuating patients under hostile fire or on adverse terrain (from rubble or from above or below ground level). (Refer to FM 8-10-6 for additional information.)

- Ensuring security measures (such as establishing checkpoints, screening personnel and vehicles, and limiting access to the MTF area) are implemented.

(4)   Medical personnel in nation assistance, support to insurgencies, and support to counter-insurgencies could be called upon to assist in the development of a MEDEVAC system. This system would provide for the supported nation/group; teach civilian, military, or paramilitary personnel basic evacuation techniques and the treatment protocols for providing en route medical care. It could also provide the more traditional support from the point of injury to the supporting treatment element.

(5)   For additional information, refer to FM 8-42.

3-11. Combat Health Support for Support Operations

a.   Support operations provide essential supplies and services to assist designated groups. They are conducted mainly to relieve suffering and help civil authorities respond to crises. In most cases, Army forces achieve success by overcoming conditions created by man-made or natural disasters. The ultimate goal of support operations is to meet the immediate needs of designated groups and transfer responsibility quickly and efficiently to appropriate civilian authorities. Support operations, which consist of humanitarian assistance and environmental assistance, accomplish one or more of the following: save lives; reduce suffering; recover essential infrastructure; improve quality of life; and restore situations to normal. The seven broad support imperatives are—

- Secure the force.

- Provide essential support to the largest number of people.

- Coordinate actions with other agencies.

- Hand over to civilian agencies as soon as feasible.

- Establish measures of success.

- Conduct robust information operations.

- Ensure operations conform to legal requirements.

b.   Humanitarian assistance operations can include a number of activities such as disaster relief, domestic support, refugee assistance, the provision of medical care to isolated populations, and refeeding programs resulting from natural or human-related disasters. Medical evacuation assets could be used to evacuate the injured from disaster sites, to provide the emergency transport of critically needed medical supplies and personnel to remote locations, or to perform emergency rescues during times of flooding, wild fires, or other natural disasters.

c.   Further, medical personnel may perform community assistance missions such as the Military Assistance to Safety and Traffic Program, where an air ambulance unit provides evacuation support to the nearby civilian community. See FM 8-42 for definitive information.

3-12. Mass Casualty Operations

Mass casualty situations occur when casualties exceed CHS capabilities. Procedures for mass casualty operations should be contained in the TSOP of each unit. Tactical standing operating procedures for mass casualty operations are coordinated through the principal staff, approved by the command, and coordinated with subordinate and higher commands. If mass casualty operations are viewed as part of area damage control missions, then the medical requirements will be integrated into the overall plan. See FMs 8-10 and 8-10-6 for definitive information.

3-13. Combat Health Support in Nuclear, Biological, and Chemical Defensive Operations

Nuclear, biological and chemical weapons of mass destruction and strategic delivery systems exist throughout the world. Delivery systems once limited to the superpowers are now available to third world nations. The corps' and division's sustainment and support capabilities are prime target for the threat's NBC weapons. The division and brigade medical units/elements can expect to conduct operations in an NBC environment. Although medical companies, platoons, or teams cannot be specifically targeted, locating close to supported CS and CSS units and near road junctions make them vulnerable to NBC weapons. Prompt notification of, and reaction to, downwind messages in the event of NBC employment will enhance both unit and individual NBC defensive measures. Defensive measures include all measures necessary to increase the effectiveness of operations, reduce the degradation to the operational tempo, and to minimize casualties. To successfully operate in a NBC environment, the DSS must focus on pre-and postdeployment training and realistic operational plans. Realistic training, SOPs considering NBC, and appropriate anticipation and preparation will greatly increase medical capability. This includes contamination avoidance and control, protection, and decontamination. Field Manuals 3-3, 3-3-1, 3-4, and 3-5 provide specific guidance for NBC avoidance and protection. For information on NBC casualty estimates, see NATO Pub AMED P-8. For definitive information on CHS in an NBC environment, see FMs 8-10-7 and 8-9. For information on NBC patient treatment, see FMs 8-9, 8-284, and 8-285.

 a.   Combat health support planning factors for NBC defensive operations include—

- Increased casualties.

- Increased MEDEVAC requirements with compromised MEDEVAC capabilities.

- Supply and resupply disruptions.

- Contamination of unit equipment, supplies, and personnel.

- Mission performance degradation due to individual protective postures.

- Prolonged treatment procedures due to decontamination.

- Increased medical treatment requirements.

- Disruption of LOC.

- Equipment damage (chemical corrosion and nuclear electromagnetic pulse).

- Select sites for medical units that are away from likely targeted areas.

- The need to adjust CHS to meet the complexities generated.

- Increased number of battle fatigue (BF) and stress-related casualties.

b.   The battlefield operations under NBC conditions can present mass casualty situations that will develop quickly and have long-lasting residual effects. The range of threat weapons, NBC weapons/agents, directed-energy weapons, and weapon delivery systems could cause high casualty rates, especially in poorly trained and improperly equipped troops and units. Medical treatment facilities could be in target areas; this will compromise medical treatment and other CHS services.

c.   The flexibility of Echelons I and II medical units and their modular design allows reconstitution of other Echelons I and II units, or the ability to task-organize to meet the CHS requirements of the supported units.

d.   The requirement for patient sorting (RTD and non-RTD [NRTD]) is of extreme importance. Many of the patients, particularly those with mild symptoms or combat stress, have excellent RTD potential. These individuals, if promptly and properly treated, could RTD within hours or a couple of days which can significantly influence the outcome of the battle. Additionally, many of these soldiers who only have BF will present physical signs and symptoms which resemble true exposure. It is important not to evacuate soldiers with minimal or no exposure to NBC hazards to hospitals. Putting BF soldiers in hospitals could reinforce their perceptions or beliefs that there is something wrong with them, other than simple fatigue and stress. It could influence their thinking and cause them to exaggerate the severity of their conditions. Also, hospitalization could slow BF soldiers' recovery and possibly result in their developing a chronic disability.

e.   Those potential RTD patients with biological or chemical effects and those with radiation exposure requiring hospitalization will be evacuated to combat support hospitals (CSHs). Restoration programs will be conducted for BF and stress-related casualties within the division. See FMs 22-51 and 8-51 for definitive information on the prevention, control, and treatment of BF and other stress-related casualties.

f.   In decontamination of NBC environments, immediate operational (individual and buddy) decontamination is absolutely critical for soldier survival. It is then essential the surgeon inform supported commanders that delaying decontamination of casualties will greatly increase their mortality and morbidity. Establishing decontamination sites, coordinating manning and training is a time-consuming task and needs to be part of the pre-operation preparation. Decontamination is the responsibility of the unit and not the medical unit. The medical unit is responsible for ensuring that the few casualties which bypass the decontamination sites are decontaminated before admission to the MTF, protecting the medical unit from contamination (verifying casualties are clean), and individual decontamination. Under medical supervision, patient decontamination is performed by nonmedical personnel from supported units. Decontamination can be greatly reduced by protecting supplies and equipment prior to attack. Surgeons can train troops to support this by integrating the training into their Combat Lifesaver Program.

3-14.   Force Protection and Security Measures

a.   Force protection is a complex process in which each action impacts upon many others. Planning for force protection is a continuous process. Force protection in stability operations and support operations scenarios can pose significant challenges.

b. The commander is responsible for providing security for his unit and the patients under his care. In some scenarios, a combat or CS unit can provide security forces to assist in the defense of medical units/elements. In other situations, the medical units/elements may not be collocated with other types of CSS units and the medical commander/leader must then provide completely for his own security. In the division, the DSMC and FSMCs are located in the DSA and BSAs with their respective battalions. The DSB and FSB commanders have the overall responsibility for the security of their battalions.

c. In stability operations and support operations, medical units could be deployed into a given geographical area prior to the deployment of combat and CS forces. During humanitarian assistance and disaster relief operations, the perceived threat may be low, but the commander must ensure that his security measures are adequate for the appropriate threat level. Further, he must ensure he has the capability to increase these protective measures should the operational scenario change and mission creep occur. If the political, social, or economic status of the HN or region deteriorates, an increase in the potential for local inhabitants to raid convoys, steal from base camps, or attack the base camp is possible. The commander must continuously evaluate the potential threat activity and adjust his force protection plan accordingly.

d. Unit and individual protective measures are discussed in detail in Joint Pub 3-07.3.

3-15. Combat Health Support Tactical Standing Operating Procedures

The DSS and the BSS are responsible for the development of the CHS annexes for the division and brigade TSOPs. The purpose of a TSOP is to establish routine protocols. The procedures in the TSOP should not be dependent upon the METT-TC factors. If a specific decision is required each time, it should not be included in the TSOP. The division and brigade surgeons assists in development of the TSOPs by their staffs and by division and brigade medical activities that include medical cells, medical platoons, and medical companies. The division and brigade TSOPs are based on the corps TSOPs and serve as the foundation for subordinate units to develop their TSOPs. The division and brigade CHS annexes to the TSOPs should be clear and concise, yet provide sufficient detail of procedural requirements. The CHS annexes to the TSOPs must reflect procedural guidance that supports current mission and doctrinal requirements. The CHS annexes to the division and brigade TSOPs should be maintained and reviewed at least every 6 months and revised as required. Most importantly, the TSOP must be trained and understood at all levels prior to deployment or it has no real value.

APPENDIX A

GUIDE FOR GENEVA CONVENTIONS COMPLIANCE

A-1. General

a. Sources for the law of war obligations of the US are customary international law and treaties ratified by the US. As such, they are part of the supreme law of the land.

b. The US is obligated to adhere to these obligations even when an opponent does not. Department of Defense and Army policy is to conduct military operations in a manner consistent with customary international law and treaty obligations.

c. An in-depth discussion of the provisions applicable to medical units and personnel is provided in FM 8-10 and FM 27-10.

A-2. Distinctive Markings and Camouflage of Medical Facilities and Evacuation Platforms

> **This paragraph implements STANAG 2027 and QSTAG 512.**

a. All US medical facilities and units, except veterinary, display the distinctive flag of the Geneva Conventions. This flag consists of a red cross on a white background. It is displayed over the unit or facility and in other places as necessary to adequately identify the unit or facility as medical.

> **This paragraph implements STANAG 2931.**

b. Camouflage of medical facilities (medical units, medical vehicles, and medical aircraft on the ground) is authorized when the lack of camouflage might compromise the tactical operation. If the failure to camouflage endangers or compromises tactical operations, the camouflage of medical facilities could be ordered by a NATO commander of at least brigade level or equivalent. Such an order is to be temporary and local in nature and is rescinded as soon as circumstances permit. It is not envisioned that large, fixed medical facilities will be camouflaged.

NOTE

As used in this context, camouflage means to cover up or remove the emblem. The black cross on an olive background is not a recognized emblem of the Geneva Conventions and is not authorized for use.

A-3. Self-Defense and Defense of Patients

Medical personnel may carry small arms for personal defense of themselves and defense of their patients. Self-defense of medical personnel or defense by medical personnel of their patients is always permitted. This does not mean that they may resist capture or otherwise fire on the advancing enemy. It means that, if civilian or enemy military personnel are attacking and ignoring the marked medical status of medical personnel, medical transportation, or the medical unit, the medical personnel may provide self-protection. If an enemy military force merely seeks to assume control of a military medical facility or a vehicle for the purpose of inspection and without firing on it, the facility or vehicle may not resist.

A-4. Enemy Prisoners of War

a. Sick, injured, or wounded EPW are treated and evacuated through medical channels, but are physically segregated from US or allied patients. The EPW patient is evacuated from the combat zone as soon as his medical condition permits.

b. Personnel resources to guard EPW patients are provided by the echelon commander. Medical personnel DO NOT guard EPW patients.

A-5. Compliance with the Geneva Conventions

a. As the US is a signatory to the Geneva Conventions, all medical personnel should thoroughly understand the provisions that apply to CHS activities. Violation of these Conventions can result in the loss of the protection afforded by them or prosecution. Medical personnel should inform the tactical commander of the consequences of violating the provisions of these Conventions.

b. The following acts are inconsistent with an individual or facility claiming protected status under the Geneva Conventions:

- Medical personnel are used to man or help man the perimeter of nonmedical facilities, such as unit trains, logistics areas, or base clusters.

- Medical personnel are used to man any offensive-type weapons or weapons systems.

- Medical personnel are ordered to engage enemy forces other than in self-defense or in the defense of patients and MTFs.

- Crew-served weapons are mounted on a medical vehicle.

- Mines or booby traps are placed in and around medical units and facilities.

- Hand grenades, light antitank weapons, grenade launchers, or any weapons other than rifles and pistols are issued to a medical unit or its personnel.

● The site of a medical unit is used as an observation post, a fuel dump, or an ammunition storage site.

c. Possible consequences of violations described in *b* above are—

● Loss of protected status for the medical unit and personnel.

● Medical facilities attacked and destroyed by the enemy.

● Medical personnel being considered prisoners of war rather than retained persons when captured.

● Combat health support capabilities decremented.

● Prosecution for violations of the law of war.

d. Other examples of violations of the Geneva Conventions include—

● Making medical treatment decisions for the wounded and sick on any basis other than medical priority, urgency, or severity of wounds.

● Allowing the interrogation of enemy wounded or sick even though medically not recommended.

● Allowing anyone to kill, torture, mistreat, or in any way harm a wounded or sick enemy soldier.

● Marking nonmedical unit facilities and vehicles with the distinctive emblem, or making any other unlawful use of this emblem.

● Using medical vehicles marked with distinctive Geneva Conventions emblem for transporting nonmedical troops, equipment, and supplies.

● Using a medical vehicle as a TOC.

e. Possible consequences of violations described in *d* above are—

● Criminal prosecution for war crimes.

● Medical personnel being considered prisoners of war rather than retained persons when captured.

NOTE

The use of smoke and obscurants by medical personnel is not a violation of the Geneva Conventions (see FMs 8-10-6 and 3-50 for information on the use of smoke).

APPENDIX B

TACTICAL STANDING OPERATING PROCEDURE

B-1.   General

All DSS and BSS must establish TSOPs. These TSOPs should be detailed and cover all aspects of division or brigade CHS operations. This is an example TSOP which can be used by both the DSS and the BSS to guide them in the development of their TSOPs.

B-2.   Sample Tactical Standing Operating Procedure

The sample shown is an annex from a division service support SOP (wartime and other operations). There is not a standard format for all TSOPs; however, it is recommended that the annex follow the format used by its higher headquarters.

**Volume II of Division Service Support Standing Operating
Procedure (WAR AND OTHER OPERATIONS)
ANNEX T (MEDICAL), ___ INFANTRY DIVISION SUPPORT COMMAND
TACTICAL STANDING OPERATING PROCEDURES**

I.   PURPOSE

This annex has been prepared to standardize operations and CHS procedures for the division in time of war and other operations.

II.   GENERAL

     A.   The division surgeon is normally located at the division main CP.

     B.   The DSS will be located with the division main CP and a DSS element deploys with the division forward TOC.

III.   ORGANIZATION AND MISSION

     A.   Medical Plans and Operations Cell. The medical plan and operations cell is responsible for—

          1.   Developing and coordinating patient evacuation support plans among the division and corps MEDEVAC elements.

          2.   Coordinating corps-level CHS for the division with the corps medical brigade/group.

          3.   Submitting A2C2 requirements for aeromedical evacuation elements to the division G3 and aviation brigade.

4.   Ensuring A2C2 information is provided to supporting corps air ambulance assets. The A2C2 information is normally provided by G3 Air at division and by the brigade S3 Air in the maneuver brigades.

5.   Coordinating aviation weather information from USAF WX detachment in the aviation brigade.

6.   Ensuring that the road clearance information provided to and received from the division MCO is disseminated to all ground ambulance assets. This information should include—

    a.   Nuclear, biological, and chemical threat.

    b.   Priorities for use of evacuation routes.

    c.   Information reported by MEDEVAC assets.

7.   Monitoring medical troop strength to determine task organization for mission accomplishment.

8.   Forwarding all medical information of potential intelligence value to the division G2 and G3 sections.

9.   Obtaining updated medical threat and intelligence information through the G2 and G3 sections for evaluation and applicability.

10.   Managing the disposition of captured medical materiels according to TSOPs.

11.   Coordinating corps CSC support to forward areas, as required.

12.   Monitoring optometry services.

B.   Combat Health Logistics Cell. The CHL cell is responsible for planning, coordinating, and prioritizing CHL and medical equipment maintenance programs for the division. The specific responsibilities of CHL cell include the following:

1.   Providing the division CHL input to the CHS plan in coordination with the DMSO.

2.   Coordinating medical maintenance training with the DMSO and supporting the MEDLOG battalion, as required.

3.   Establishing maintenance priorities for repair and exchange of medical equipment (this is coordinated by the MMMB).

4.   Ensuring that a viable preventive maintenance program is established and monitored.

5. Coordinating the evacuation and replacement of medical equipment with the supporting MEDLOG company.

6. Verifying emergency supply requests for submission to the corps MEDLOG company and taking the necessary action to expedite shipment.

7. Analyzing Class VIII resupply operations, identifying trends in performance, and coordinating with the MEDLOG company/battalion any changes that would enhance the Class VIII delivery system.

8. Establishing and managing, in coordination with the division and brigade surgeons, the medical critical items list.

9. Interfacing with the MCO to ensure necessary coordination with the division supply and transportation system occurs.

10. Establishing transportation procedures, based on the tactical situation, with the MMMB and MEDLOG company/battalion.

11. Providing technical staff assistance for the MMMB, as required, to ensure divisionwide support for CHL and blood management.

12. Establishing coordination procedures for the disposition of captured medical materiel.

C. Responsibilities of the Patient Disposition and Reports Cell. The patient disposition and reports cell is responsible for coordinating patient disposition throughout the division. The branch obtains and coordinates disposition of patients with the medical plans and operations cell and the corps MRO. It prepares and forwards appropriate medical statistical reports as required.

D. Preventive Medicine Cell. The division PVNTMED cell is responsible for supervising the command PVNTMED program according to the division CHS plan and AR 40-5. The PVNTMED cell is staffed to provide advice and consultation in the areas of environmental sanitation, epidemiology environmental surveillance, entomology, and sanitary engineering services. The primary mission of the PVNTMED cell is to protect division personnel against food-, water-, vectorborne diseases, as well as environmental injuries by implementing preventive measures. All PVNTMED missions are coordinated by the PVNTMED officer through the medical plan/operations cell. Additional information pertaining to the PVNTMED cell and its specific functions is discussed in FMs 8-10, 8-10-1, 8-10-3, and 4-02.17 (8-10-17).

IV. ECHELON II COMBAT HEALTH SUPPORT

A. The division provides Echelon II medical treatment, and evacuation. Class VIII resupply for the division medical elements is supported by the MEDLOG company using throughput resupply system to the FSMCs and the DSMC. One FSMC operates in DS of each maneuver brigade and locates an MTF in the BSA of the supported brigade. The DSMC locates and establishes an MTF in the DSA.

B.   Combat health support is provided on an area support basis to nondivisional units operating within the division AO.

V.   MEDICAL EVACUATION

A.   General.

1.   Evacuation is based on the principle that rear higher echelon medical units are responsible for evacuating patients from supported units. Lower echelon supported and supporting units must ensure evacuation support plans are complete and current by close, direct coordination. See FM 8-10-6 for an in-depth discussion of MEDEVAC; for additional information, refer to FMs 8-10, 8-10-1, 8-10-4, 4-02.24 (8-10-24), 8-42, 8-55, 63-20, and 63-21.

2.   Patients are evacuated no further to the rear than that necessary to obtain the medical care which will return them to duty. Patients are evacuated by the means of transportation that most clearly meets the treatment demands of their wounds, injury, or illness.

3.   Allied military personnel, treated or held in a division MTF within reasonable proximity of their own national facility, are classified and processed as follows:

a.   Allied military personnel requiring further treatment, but in stable condition for immediate transfer, are returned to their own national medical facility, as coordinated through liaison with the corps or division surgeon.

b.   Allied military personnel requiring further stabilization are retained in US medical channels until they can be safely transferred to their own national MTFs. Complete arrangements for reception of the patient by the gaining MTF are completed prior to the evacuation.

c.   The preferred method for evacuation of neuropsychiatric (NP) and BF casualties who can be managed without medications or physical restraints is a nonambulance ground vehicle. If physical restraints and/or medications are required during transportation, ground ambulance is preferred. An air ambulance should only be used if no other means of evacuation is available. Physical restraints are used only during transport and medications are given only if needed for reasons of safety. Those NP/BF patients with life- or limb-threatening conditions are evacuated by the most expedient means available. If evacuation is by air ambulance, physical restraints will be used. See FMs 8-10-6 and 8-51.

d.   Patients are not held longer than 72 hours in the division holding elements of the MTFs. If patients cannot be treated and returned to duty within 72 hours, they are evacuated as soon as possible.

B.   Control of Property and Equipment.

1.   Soldiers evacuated from Echelon I medical elements will be transported to the next higher (Echelon II) MTF with their protective mask and clothing only.

2. Any property and equipment arriving with casualties other than the protective mask and clothing at the FSMC will be collected and turned into the parent unit for final disposition. The FSB S4 coordinates the return of property and equipment to the casualty's unit.

3. Under combat conditions, protective masks are kept in the immediate proximity of each patient throughout their period of evacuation and stay at MTFs. In other operations the protective mask policy for patients will be based on the NBC threat and the policy established by higher headquarters.

C. Medical Evacuation In the Division.

1. Ground evacuation is considered the primary means of evacuation in the combat zone under most scenarios. However, due to the limited numbers of available air ambulances, medical planners should plan to use air ambulances for urgent and urgent surgical category patients. Ground MEDEVAC will be accomplished by supporting ambulance element; however, in emergencies any military vehicle could be used to transport a casualty to the nearest MTF.

2. When dedicated MEDEVAC means are not available, nonmedical ground/air assets will be used to backhaul casualties to MTFs. The FSC medical platoon in support of a maneuver battalion will provide ground ambulance evacuation from the maneuver elements back to the BAS. Company aid posts and patient collecting points will be established as part of the battalion medical support plan. The medical platoon/section of separate battalions attached to the brigade will receive ambulance support on an area basis. The ambulance platoon also provides area support ambulance coverage for the BSA.

3. The ambulance platoon of the FSMC will provide ground ambulance support from the BAS operated by the medical platoons of the FSCs back to the BSA. It also provides area support ambulance support for the BSA. The ambulance platoon of the division support medical company provides area support ambulance coverage for the DSA and supporting corps units attached/OPCON to the division.

4. Attached/OPCON corps air ambulance will be pre-positioned in the division. Air ambulances that are positioned in the BSAs will provide MEDEVAC from the forward areas back to the FSMC. Medical evacuation by air ambulance is normally accomplished for urgent and urgent surgical category patients. Air ambulance evacuation from point of injury is METT-TC dependent. Corps air ambulances positioned in the DSA or those dispatched from the corps area will be tasked with MEDEVAC from the BSAs and DSA to corps CSHs. Corps ground ambulances will provide MEDEVAC from the BSAs and DSA to the corps CSHs.

D. Rules for Employment of Ambulance and Ambulance Personnel.

1. The use of MEDEVAC vehicles will be restricted to—

   a. Transportation of sick or injured personnel.

   b. Transportation of medical personnel.

   c. Transportation of Class VIII supplies/equipment and blood.

2. Medical personnel assigned to the ambulances will—

   a. Adhere to the tactical commanders' standards for uniform and camouflage and other requirements identified in the supported unit's TSOP.

   b. Participate in the medical training being conducted at the supported medical element.

   c. Assist with patient treatment as required.

NOTE

Caution should be exercised by officers in charge or noncommissioned officers in charge to ensure the ambulance crew has adequate rest in order that they can safely perform their evacuation duties.

   d. Perform PMCS on their vehicles.

   e. Ensure their vehicle is restocked with required Class VIII supplies, full of fuel, and ready for the next evacuation mission.

3. Medical personnel assigned to the ambulances which are positioned with the supported medical element will not—

   a. Be required to perform duties as kitchen police (KP), EPW or perimeter guards, or drivers of other than their assigned vehicle.

   b. Violate the provisions of the Geneva Conventions.

E. Use of Aeromedical Evacuation.

1. Aeromedical evacuation is the preferred method of evacuation and will routinely be used when—

   a. Life, limb, or eyesight is in jeopardy (urgent or urgent surgical category).

   b. Speed, distance, and time are factors in assuring prompt and adequate treatment.

   c. There is a critical need for resupply of Class VIII supplies or whole blood/blood products.

   d. There is a critical need for movement of medical personnel and equipment.

2.   Helicopter LZs are established when and where tactical situations permit. A helicopter LZ should be marked with a letter "H" or a letter "Y," using identification panels or other appropriate marking material. See FMs 8-10-6 and 57-38 for a complete description and guidelines for establishing a helicopter LZ.

3.   Precedence for air ambulance evacuation is provided in FM 8-10-6.

VI.   DECEASED PERSONNEL

A.   Principles Governing Medical Disposition of Deceased Personnel.

1.   Deceased personnel are segregated from other casualties.

2.   The deceased, as determined by the senior medical authority, are not evacuated with other casualties nor are they routinely evacuated on medical vehicles. Especially if the threat of biological or chemical contamination will render the vehicle unfit for subsequent MEDEVAC missions. A US Field Medical Card (FMC), DD Form 1380, should be initiated and attached to the remains, if possible.

3.   All casualties requiring medical treatment are evacuated prior to transporting any deceased personnel.

4.   Medical evacuation resources should not be used to transport deceased personnel.

5.   All deceased personnel should have an FMC that is signed by a medical officer prior to their departure from a graves registration collection point operating in forward areas.

B.   Use/Nonuse of Principles Governing Medical Disposition of Deceased Personnel.

1.   These principles are not an absolute.

2.   Field commanders should have an understanding of the rationale behind the above principles when making command decisions pertaining to deceased personnel.

VII.   ENEMY PRISONERS OF WAR

A.   All EPW will be provided medical care according to the articles of the Geneva Convention for the Amelioration of the Condition of the Wounded and Sick in Armed Forces in the Field, dated 12 August 1949.

B.   Enemy prisoner of war patients will be segregated from US and allied personnel.

C.   Enemy prisoner of war patients will be reported through normal medical reporting procedures.

D.   Enemy medical personnel are considered retained personnel and shall receive the benefits provided by the Geneva Conventions.   Retained enemy medical personnel will be used to the maximum extent possible to care and treat EPW patients.

E.   Enemy prisoner of war patients will be evacuated through medical channels.

F.   Enemy prisoner of war patients will be under armed guard at all times.   Guards are the responsibility of the echelon commander.   Medical personnel will not be used as guards for EPW according to the Geneva Conventions.

G.   Enemy prisoner of war patients will be searched prior to each move in the MEDEVAC system.

H.   Information on EPW patients will be coordinated with the prisoner of war information center to maintain accountability of captives in medical channels.   See FM 19-4 for additional information on EPWs.

VIII.   CLASS VIII SUPPLY

A.   The medical platoon of the FSCs will digitally request Class VIII resupply as a passing action through their FSMC from MEDLOG company.

B.   Forward support medical companies will request Class VIII resupply from the MEDLOG company.

C.   Property exchange will be accomplished for all medical materiel (litters, evacuation bags, wool blankets, IV stands, and splints) accompanying patients during evacuation.

D.   The MMMB coordinates throughput Class VIII resupply for the division. Maximum use of air and ground ambulances moving forward, should be used to carry Class VIII resupply and replacement medical personnel.

E.   Medical maintenance will consist of—

1.   Operator/user-level maintenance which requires that medical personnel exercise their responsibilities by performing operator PMCS, to include—

a.   Maintaining equipment by performing routine services like cleaning, dusting, washing, and checking for frayed cables, loose hardware, and cracked or rotting seals.

b.   Performing equipment operational testing.

c.   Replacing operator-level spares and repair parts that will not require extensive disassembly of the end item, critical adjustment after the replacement, or extensive use of tools.

    d. Annotating appropriate documentation.

    2. Division medical equipment repairers will exercise their responsibilities by—

    a. Scheduling and performing their PMCS functions, electrical safety inspections and tests, and calibration, verification, and certification services.

    b. Performing unscheduled maintenance functions with emphasis upon the component-level repairs and replacement of assemblies, modules, and printed circuit boards.

    c. Conducting a medical equipment repair parts program.

    d. Maintaining a technical library of operator and maintenance TMs and/or associated manufacturers' manuals.

    e. Conducting inspections for new or transferred equipment.

    f. Maintaining documentation of maintenance functions in accordance with the provisions of TB 38-750-2 or the DA standard automated system.

    g. Collecting and reporting data for readiness reportable medical equipment according to AR 700-138.

    h. Notifying the supporting MEDLOG company of requirements for maintaining support services, repairable exchange, or replacement from the MEDSTEP (see AR 40-61).

IX. BLOOD MANAGEMENT POLICIES AND PROCEDURES

    A. Responsibilities.

    1. The division surgeon is ultimately responsible for the division's blood program.

    2. The DSS, in coordination with the division surgeon, is responsible for the overall planning and execution of the division's blood program.

    3. The HSMO of the CHL cell monitors and coordinates the division blood program. The HSMO, in coordination with the DISCOM MMMB, is responsible for managing blood inventory levels and ordering blood for the division.

    4. Medical company commanders, through their treatment platoon leaders, monitor blood usage and inventory levels.

    5. The medical laboratory specialists of each area support treatment squad are the technical advisors to the medical company commanders and treatment platoon leaders on all matters pertaining to the blood program.

6.   Each medical company will maintain an inventory of 50 units of Group O packed red blood cells for wartime operations. In other operations, the division surgeon will establish inventory levels. The blood support detachment will maintain 30 to 50 units of Group O packed red cells for each medical company supported. Blood stockage levels will be adjusted as necessary to meet division blood requirements.

B.   Delivery of Blood.

1.   Blood will be shipped by air when circumstances permit. Unless otherwise specified, 15 percent of the blood requested should be Rh negative. During shipment, blood will be continuously maintained at a temperature within the range of 1 degree to 10 degrees Centigrade.

2.   Blood still on hand 5 days before the expiration date will be kept properly refrigerated and returned to the blood support detachment.

C.   Blood Management Report.

1.   Depending on the tactical situation and the command policy, the blood report (BLDREP) could be transmitted by voice or written means (transmitted electronic message, telephonically, or by courier).

2.   Medical companies will submit their requirements for the following day and the status of blood on hand to the blood support detachment with information copies to the DSS and brigade surgeon. Medical companies will consolidate and submit requirements according to timelines provided by higher headquarters.

X.   MANAGEMENT OF MASS CASUALTIES

A.   Mass casualty situations occur when the number of casualties exceed the available medical capability to rapidly treat and evacuate them. The surgeon working with the G4 and the G3 advises the commander on integrating all available resources into an effective mass casualty plan.

B.   All division medical companies must have procedures in place to respond effectively to mass casualty situations. The potential of disasters in war and other operations require that division medical companies be prepared to support mass casualty situations. They must be able to receive, triage, treat, and evacuate large numbers of casualties within a short period of time. Contingency plans for supporting mass casualty operations must be developed by all division medical companies in coordination with their battalion S3. Unit mass casualty plans, as a minimum, will address the following subject areas:

1.   Planning and training requirements.

2.   Medical duty positions.

3.   Nonmedical personnel positions and duties, including litter teams, perimeter guards crowd control, and information personnel.

4. Location of treatment areas, to include triage, immediate care, minimal care, delayed care, and expectant care areas.

5. Support requirements beyond the unit's capability.

6. Medical evacuation.

7. Use of nonmedical transportation assets.

8. Nuclear, biological, and chemical casualties.

9. Return to duty procedures.

10. Medical records and reports.

11. Locating deceased personnel away from and out of sight of all patients.

C. The DSS or brigade surgeons' sections should be informed of any mass casualty situation by the most expedient means available. As a minimum, information provided should include location, anticipated number of casualties, and additional support required.

D. The DSS directs and coordinates CHS requirements for the requesting unit. Supporting corps and division medical units in the chain of evacuation are alerted of the situation.

XI. PREVENTIVE MEDICINE

A. The division PVNTMED cell will oversee all PVNTMED activities in the division.

B. The PVNTMED cell is responsible for supervising the division's PVNTMED program as described in AR 40-5. This cell ensures PVNTMED measures are implemented to protect division personnel against food-, water-, and arthropodborne diseases, as well as environmental injuries (for example, heat and cold injuries). This cell provides advice and consultation in the areas of environmental sanitation, epidemiology, sanitary engineering, and pest management.

C. Preventive medicine personnel will conduct evaluations to identify actual and potential health hazards, recommend corrective measures, and assist in training personnel in disease prevention programs.

D. Preventive medicine support is requested through the DSS or brigade surgeons' sections and formal tasking is accomplished through the division or brigade headquarters.

E. All deployable company size units in the division will establish unit field sanitation teams. Preventive medicine personnel will assist in the training of these teams in the aspects of environmental sanitation and the limited control of animal reservoirs and disease vectors.

F.   Company/battery/troop commanders will—

1.   Use trained field sanitation team members on all field exercises to assist in preserving the health of the unit and reducing the incidence of DNBI which will hinder mission accomplishment (FM 21-10).

2.   Ensure the field sanitation team members take to the field all required field sanitation equipment and supplies to perform their duty (AR 40-5).

3.   Enforce food and water safety standards. Unless otherwise stated, water will be treated to at least 5 parts per million chloride residual and will be obtained from approved sources only. Safe handling, storage, and preparation of food will be according to AR 30-21, AR 40-5, and FM 21-10.

4.   Plan for the construction of hygienic devices, such as handwashing devices in the unit area. They will also enforce personal hygiene measures to reduce the threat of disease.

5.   Motivate subordinates to execute individual preventive measures (such as carrying an extra pair of dry socks; and/or eating or drinking from approved sources only).

6.   Enforce the use of the DOD repellent systems requiring the use of repellents on skin (DEET [75 percent N, N-diethyl-M-toluamide]) and clothing (permethrin).

7.   Develop and enforce the unit sleep plan that provides soldiers with a minimum of 4 hours of uninterrupted sleep in a 24-hour period. If sleep is interrupted, then 5 hours should be given. During continuous operations when uninterrupted sleep is not possible, blocks of sleep which add up to 6 hours in a 24-hour period are adequate for most people. Remember, 4 hours each 24-hour period is far from ideal. Do not go with only 4 hours sleep each 24 hours for more than 2 weeks before paying back sleep debt. Recovery time should be approximately 8-10 hours sleep each 24 hours over a 5 to 7 day period. If at all possible, give 6 hours of sleep a day to those individuals (such as ambulance drivers) whose key tasks are vulnerable to sleep loss.

8.   Plan for measures to prevent environmental injuries (such as heat or cold) (see FM 21-10).

9.   Obtain and disseminate information on the medical threat so soldiers can reduce their risk of DNBIs.

10.   Request PVNTMED consultation/assistance. Requests can be submitted to the DSS, the brigade surgeon's section, or any medical company/element in the division.

XII.   DIVISION DENTAL SERVICES

A.   Dental treatment facilities are located in each FSMC and in the support medical company. Each medical company establishes dental sick call hours; supported units are notified of the sick call hours available.

B.   The division dental surgeon (appointed by division surgeon) establishes policies and procedures for dental services in the division. He plans and supervises the preventive dentistry program for the division according to AR 40-35.

C.   In wartime operations, division dental services are limited to emergency, preventive, and general dental care (see FM 8-10-19).

D.   In other operations, dental services are METT-TC driven; however, as a minimum, include emergency and preventive dental care. In other operation scenarios, general dental care is provided in the division.

E.   Dental personnel will assist medical treatment personnel in mass casualty situations.

XIII.   DIVISION MENTAL HEALTH/COMBAT STRESS CONTROL

A.   Under the guidance of the division psychiatrist (assigned to the DSMC) CSC teams assigned to division medical companies provide mental health/CSC services. Responsibilities for the NP/CSC personnel include—

1.   Monitoring indicators of dysfunctional stress in units.

2.   Evaluating NP, BF, and misconduct stress behavior cases.

3.   Providing consultation and triage as requested for medical/surgical patients exhibiting signs of combat stress or NP disorders.

4.   Supervising selective short-term restoration for HOLD category BF casualties (1 to 3 days).

5.   Coordinating support activities of attached corps-level CSC elements. A CSC team is assigned to each medical company to provide CSC support for each of the maneuver brigade. The division psychiatrist has technical control over all division mental health/CSC staff. The division psychiatrist is responsible for supervising, coordinating, and requesting additional mental health/CSC support for the division as required.

B.   The division psychiatrist, assisted by mental health/CSC personnel, prepare mental health/ CSC estimates as directed or required to support CHS operations. These mental health/CSC estimates will pertain to the following subject areas:

1.   Mental health status of the division.

2.   Current status of morale and unit cohesion in division units.

3.   Battle fatigue casualty estimates.

4. Effects of fatigue and sleep loss.

5. Percent of casualties; intensity of combat.

6. Home-front stressors (natural disaster, unpopular support of the conflict, and terrorist attack in or around home base).

7. Restoration requirements.

8. Corps CSC support requirements.

9. Coordination of consultations (critical events debriefings) following critical events such as a fatal accident, rear battle incident, or other catastrophic event.

C. The division psychiatric or mental health staff should be consulted prior to the evacuation of NP patients from the division.

XIV. OPTOMETRY SERVICE

A. The optometry section is organic to the DSMC.

B. Optometry services in the division include—

1. Routine vision evaluation and refractions.

2. Evaluation and management of ocular injuries and disease.

3. Spectacle frame assembly using presurfaced single-vision lenses.

4. Spectacle repair services for units within the division AO.

C. The optometry officer will advise commanders as required on all matters relating to vision, to include protective eyewear (ballistic and laser protection).

D. This section ensures that division procedures are established for personnel who require optometry services. These procedures should include the following:

1. Each soldier requiring prescription eyewear deploying with two pair plus inserts for protective mask.

2. Personnel authorized to wear contact lenses deploying with two pairs of standard eyewear.

3. Supporting optometry section maintaining a copy of the most recent prescription for each soldier assigned to the division.

4.   Soldiers requiring optometry services being referred from their supporting MTF.

5.   Eyewear that is broken or in need of repair being sent to the MEDLOG company for repair or replacement.

6.   Request for replacement of lost eyewear being forwarded to the MEDLOG company.

XV.   GENEVA CONVENTIONS COMPLIANCE

A.   Medical Facilities.

1.   All US medical facilities and units, except veterinary, will display the distinctive flag of the Geneva Conventions. This flag consists of a red cross on a white background. It is displayed over the unit or facility and in other places as necessary to adequately identify the unit or facility. Nondisplay of the flag can be ordered by a brigade or higher level commander.

2.   Camouflage of the medical facility (medical units, medical vehicle, and medical aircraft on the ground) is authorized when a lack of camouflage might compromise the tactical operation.

3.   The order to camouflage can be given by a brigade-level or higher commander.

NOTE

As used in this context, camouflage means to cover up or remove the Geneva Conventions emblem. The black cross on an olive background is not a recognized emblem of the Geneva Conventions.

B.   Defense of Medical Units.

1.   Medical personnel may carry small arms for personal defense of themselves and defense of their patients. Self-defense of medical personnel or defense by medical personnel of their patients is always permitted. This does not mean that they may resist capture or otherwise fire on the advancing enemy. It means that, if civilian or enemy military personnel are attacking and ignoring the marked medical status of medical personnel, medical transportation, or the medical unit, the medical personnel may provide self-protection. If an enemy military force merely seeks to assume control of a military medical facility or a vehicle for the purpose of inspection and without firing on it, the facility or vehicle may not resist.

2.   An overall defense plan may not require medical units to take offensive or defensive actions against enemy troop at any time. If a medical force is part of a defensive area containing nonmedical units, medical personnel may not be responsible for manning part of the overall perimeter. If located in isolation, the medical unit may provide its own local and internal security if other support is not available. However, all soldiers (medical and nonmedical) providing this internal and local security must comply with the requirements in subparagraph 1 above.

XVI. MEDICAL REPORTING

A. Field Medical Card. The FMC will be initiated for each new patient and for cases required to be carded for record only. This will be accomplished according to AR 40-66 and FMs 8-10-6 and 8-230. Field Medical Cards will be conspicuously attached to the patient's clothing.

B. Daily Disposition Log (DDL). The DDL is maintained by all Echelon I and Echelon II MTFs assigned or attached to the division. Information from this log is extracted, when required, and provided to the S1 or the supported unit requesting the information. The DDL is also the primary source document for information needed in the preparation of the Patient Summary Report (PSR) and the Patient Evacuation and Mortality Report (PE&MR). See Appendix 1 for a sample format.

C. Medical Reports Format. Medical reporting will be accomplished using the FBCB2, FAX or voice, transmitted via radio/MSE. A manual backup system will be developed. Formats for medical reports are required to maintain consistency and continuity in reporting procedures for information submitted to the BSS and the DSS. Data contained in these reports are required to support the DSS's capability projections and to assist the BSS, HSSO, and FSMC commander in coordinating and planning CHS operations. Data is also extracted for consolidated reporting to higher headquarters. The guidelines presented below should be followed exactly.

1. Each line of information is divided into a number of fields. Each field has a minimum number of alphanumeric characters as indicated in the sample format provided (see Appendix 2).

2. Each field is separated by a single slash(/).

3. The end of each set of fields is indicated by a double Slash (//).

4. If information from a prior report has not changed, "NC" will be entered in that field (/NC/).

5. Reports are formatted according to special instructions and reports format. A sample message is provided with each appendix.

D. Medical Situation Report, Battalion Aid Station. The Medical Situation Report, BAS, is a daily patient summary report. This report is used to inform the commander of the battalion's patient, Class VIII, and medical equipment status. This report is submitted daily, covering the events in a 24-hour time period based on timelines provided by the higher headquarters. It is submitted to the supporting medical company. The battalion surgeon (platoon leader) or platoon sergeant is responsible for this report. This report could be dispatched via courier, FAX, and/or teletype. See Appendix 2 for a sample format.

E. Medical Situation Report, Medical Companies. The Medical Situation Report, Medical Companies, is a daily patient summary report. This report is submitted daily to the DSS according to time-lines provided by higher headquarters. The following information will be included in line six of this report:

1. Status of all assigned and attached ambulances, to include—

a. Total number of ambulances.

b.   Number of ambulances that are operational.

c.   Number of ambulances that are nonoperational.

2.   Status of personnel; identify shortages by AOC or MOS.

3.   Treatment of any EPW will be entered in this section.

4.   Identify all patients seen during the reporting period with a number and provide the following information in the order provided below:

a.   Nationality.

b.   Name.

c.   Rank.

d.   Service number.

e.   Unit.

f.   Date of birth.

g.   Diagnosis.

h.   Disposition.

i.   Date of disposition.

j.   Gaining unit.

5.   A hard copy of each aid station's Medical Situation Report must accompany the submitting medical company's report.   See Appendix 3 for a sample format.

F.   Medical Situation Report, Medical Operations.   The Medical Situation Report, Medical Operations, is a consolidated patient summary report.   This report is consolidated by the DSS and pertains to the previous 24 hours.   It is submitted from the DSS daily to the division based on timelines established by the division surgeon.   See Appendix 4 for a sample format.

G.   Patient Evacuation and Mortality Report.   All Echelons I and II MTFs assigned or attached to the division prepare the PE&MR.   The purpose of this report is to provide a status of patients seen by division MTFs.   This is a weekly report compiled as of 2400 each Sunday and distributed each Monday to supported units.   See Appendix 5 for a sample format.

H.   Patient Summary Report.   The PSR provides the status of patients seen by division medical companies and includes their subordinate elements (dental, optometry, mental health, or attached units).

The PSR is a weekly report compiled as of 2400 each Sunday. It is prepared by all Echelons I and II MTFs operating in the division AO. It is submitted each Monday to the DSS. See Appendix 6 for a sample format.

     I.   Blood Report. The Blood Report is a required report for requesting blood support. Echelon II MTFs will request only Group O Positive and Group O Negative liquid red blood cells. See Appendix 7 for sample formats (Sample Format A for written blood report and Sample Format B for voice message format).

     J.   Team Movement Report. The Team Movement Report is used to track the status and location of teams (PVNTMED, combat stress, veterinary, ambulance, and treatment teams). See Appendix 8 for a sample format.

APPENDIX 1

SAMPLE FORMAT (DAILY DISPOSITION LOG)
TO ANNEX T, MEDICAL REPORTS

_____ INF DIV TSOP

DAILY DISPOSITION LOG

DATE-TIME GROUP (DTG): _____

NAME	GRADE	SSN	UNIT/NATION	INJURY/ILLNESS STATUS	DISPOSITION TIME
SHAW, L.	O3	000000000	A TRP RECON	GSW, L-LEG/WIA	CLR-0900Z
HERRERA, C.	E4	000000000	C3, 6 INF/US	SICK/MIGRAINE/DIS	RTD-1400Z
JONES, C.J.	E6	000000000	A1, 6 INF/US	LACERATION-L HAND/NBI	CLR-1200Z
EPW (UNKNOWN)			EPW	FRAG WOUND OF HEAD/DOA/KIA	MA-1220Z
IVANOVICH, N.	O4	000000000	EPW	SW R-ARM/WIA	MP/BDE SCTY ELEM 1400Z
FLOWERS, R.C.	E8	000000000	B TRP RECON SQDN/US	BF/DNBI	CLR-1640Z
CONRAD, W.	E5	000000000	6 PANZER/GE	BURN, 3D DEGREE CHEST/ABDOMEN/WIA	CLR-1400Z
DECK, H.	O2	000000000	C BTRY, 3 FA/US	PUNCTURE WOUND R-ANKLE/WIA	CLR-1400Z
HASLEY, B.	E1	000000000	B TRP RECON SQDN/US	CHEMICAL INJ SYSTEMIC/WIA	28TH FLD-1705Z
WATSON, WM. T.	E3	000000000	B TRP RECON SQDN/US	DE INJ BOTH EYES	28TH FLD-1815Z
FISHER, T.T.	E7	000000000	A TRP RECON SQDN/US	UNCONTROLLED VOMITING-BW/WIA	CLR-1900Z

NOTE: THIS LOG, IN THE ABOVE FORMAT, IS MAINTAINED BY ALL DIVISIONAL TREATMENT FACILITIES. IT DOES NOT LEND ITSELF FOR TRANSMISSION. HOWEVER, THE INFORMATION MAY BE EXTRACTED AND PROVIDED TO AGENCIES RESPONSIBLE FOR PREPARING THE CONSOLIDATED FEEDER REPORT.

LEGEND:

BDE	BRIGADE	DTG	DATE-TIME GROUP	L	LEFT
BF	BATTLE FATIGUE	ELEM	ELEMENT	MA	MORTUARY AFFAIRS
BW	BIOLOGICAL WARFARE	FA	FIELD ARTILLERY	MP	MILITARY POLICE
CLR	CLEARING (STATION)	FRAG	FRAGMENTATION (WOUND)	NBI	NONBATTLE INJURY
DE	DIRECTED ENERGY	GE	GERMAN	R	RIGHT
DIS	DISEASE	GSW	GUN SHOT WOUND	RECON	RECONNAISSANCE
DNBI	DISEASE AND NONBATTLE INJURY (PURPLE HEART NOT AUTHORIZED)	INF	INFANTRY	SCTY	SECURITY
		INJ	INJURY	SQDN	SQUADRON
		KIA	KILLED IN ACTION (PURPLE HEART AUTHORIZED)	TRP	TROOP
DOA	DEAD ON ARRIVAL			US	UNITED STATES
				WIA	WOUNDED IN ACTION (PURPLE HEART AUTHORIZED)

APPENDIX 2

SAMPLE FORMAT (MEDICAL SITUATION REPORT, BATTALION AID STATION) TO ANNEX T, MEDICAL REPORTS

_____ INF DIV TSOP

FM: BAS

TO: BSS//

INFO: FSB/FSMC // DSS (AS APPROPRIATE) //

CLASSIFICATION: (AS APPROPRIATE)

SUBJECT: MEDICAL SITUATION REPORT (BAS)

LINE ONE   AS OF DTG IN ZULU TIME

LINE TWO   LOCATION (SIX DIGIT GRID COORDINATES)

LINE THREE   NUMBER OF PATIENTS SEEN (INCLUDING TYPE OF PATIENTS [W=WIA, D=DNBI])

LINE FOUR   NUMBER OF PATIENTS RETURNED TO DUTY

LINE FIVE   NUMBER OF PATIENTS EVACUATED FROM BATTLE AREA

LINE SIX   NUMBER OF PATIENTS AWAITING EVACUATION

LINE SEVEN   NUMBER OF OPERATIONAL AMBULANCES BY TYPE OF VEHICLE (M996, M113)

LINE EIGHT   LOGISTIC STATUS (GREEN, AMBER, OR RED)/USE REPORT CODES IN APPENDIX 9

APPENDIX 3

**SAMPLE FORMAT (MEDICAL SITUATION REPORT, MEDICAL COMPANY)
TO ANNEX T, MEDICAL REPORTS**

_____ **INF DIV TSOP**

FM: FSMC COMMANDER
TO: BRIGADE SURGEON'S SECTION
INFO: FSB COMMANDER

CLASSIFICATION: (AS APPROPRIATE)
SUBJECT: MEDICAL SITUATION REPORT

LINE ONE:	AS OF: DTG IN ZULU TIME
LINE TWO:	PATIENT STATUS (WIA, DNBI) UNIT DESIGNATION//** TOTAL NEW PATIENTS SEEN/CONSOLIDATED BY EACH FSMC (AS TOTAL [W=,D=]) FSB (W=,D=)/PNT RTD (BAS TOTAL= +FSB=#//TOTAL # PATIENTS EVACUATED TO BDE REAR(DSA=#, TO CORPS)//# OF NEW PATIENT HOLDING// END OF DAY HOLDING CENSUS
LINE THREE:	UNIT STATUS
	**6 DIGIT COORDINATES//# OF COTS AVAILABLE FOR HOLDING//# OF COTS OCCUPIED//# OF COTS UPLOADED ON VEHICLE, TIME NEEDED TO GET HOLDING AREA OPERATIONAL
	**INDICATES THAT OPERATIONAL COTS ARE ASSEMBLED AND READY FOR PATIENTS
LINE FOUR	ANTICIPATED UNIT MOVE IN NEXT 24 HOURS; IF NONE, REPORT "0" UNIT//ANTICIPATED NEW LOCATION//ANTICIPATED TIME BECOMING OPERATIONAL (DTG)//*PROJECTED NUMBER OF PATIENTS REQUIRING EVACUATION TO REAR
LINE FIVE	HEALTH SERVICE LOGISTICS
	**GREEN, AMBER, OR RED
	**DENOTES MEDICAL PERSONNEL MAKING DETERMINATION OF COLOR STATUS BY UNIT STOCKAGE LEVEL AND PROJECTED OPERATIONS. CLARIFY ALL AMBER AND RED STATUS IN REMARKS. GREEN=80-100%; AMBER=65-80%; RED=LESS THAN 65% OF INITIAL STOCKAGE LEVEL
LINE SIX	EVACUATION ASSETS
	NUMBER OF AMBULANCES OPERATIONAL IN BSA/DSA
LINE SEVEN	INCLUDE # OF NBC PATIENTS//# OF EPW PATIENTS// PERSONNEL SHORTAGES//MAJOR END ITEM SHORTAGES (BASIS FOR LINE FIVE STATUS)
USE	REPORT CODES IN APPENDIX 9

APPENDIX 4

**SAMPLE FORMAT (MEDICAL SITUATION REPORT, MEDICAL OPERATIONS)
TO ANNEX T, MEDICAL REPORTS**

_____ INF DIV TSOP

FM: 1ST BDE SURGEON'S SECTION
TO: DIVISION SURGEON'S SECTION

INFORMATION: NONE

CLASSIFICATION: AS APPROPRIATE

SUBJECT: COMBAT HEALTH SUPPORT SITUATION REPORT

LINE ONE: AS OF: DTG IN ZULU TIME

LINE TWO: PATIENT STATUS
TOTAL NEW PATIENTS W-#, D=#//NUMBER OF RTD//# OF PATIENTS
EVACUATED TO CORPS//# OF NEW PATIENTS IN HOLDING STATUS//END
OF DAY HOLDING STATUS CENSUS

LINE THREE: UNIT STATUS
*UNIT DESIGNATION//6 DIGIT GRID COORDINATES//# OF OPERATIONAL
COTS//# OF UNOCCUPIED COTS//# OF COTS UPLOADED ON VEHICLES,
TIME NEEDED TO BE OPERATIONAL

*ONE PARAGRAPH FOR EACH FSMC ASSIGNED OR ATTACHED TO THE
DIVISION AND ONE FOR THE SUPPORT MED COMPANY. TO BE REPORT-
ED AS ALPHA, BRAVO, CHARLIE, ETC

LINE FOUR: ANTICIPATED OPERATIONS IN NEXT 24 HOURS; IF ONE, STATE UNIT
DESIGNATION//ANTICIPATED DTG CLOSING TIME (NONOPERATIONAL)//
ANTICIPATED NEW LOCATION//ANTICIPATED OPERATIONAL TIME//

LINE FIVE: COMBAT HEALTH LOGISTICS
UNIT ID WITH AMBER OR RED//UNIT ID WITH AMBER OR RED, STATUS
LEVEL (AMBER OR RED)

APPENDIX 5

SAMPLE FORMAT (PATIENT EVACUATION AND MORTALITY REPORT)
TO ANNEX T, MEDICAL REPORTS

_____ INF DIV TSOP

PATIENT EVACUATION AND MORTALITY REPORT

DATE-TIME GROUP (DTG): _____

(FROM) / (TO)

ALPHA (EVACUATED)

NAME	GRADE	SSN	*UNIT/NATION	TENTATIVE DIAGNOSIS	DESTINATION DTG
WILSON, V.C.	03	000000000	A TRP RECON SQDN/US	MULTIPLE GSWs ABDOMEN AND L-THIGH	28TH FLD/ 251015Z MAR 86
NELSON, B.	05	000000000	HHC, CAB 71D/US	FUO	15TH CSH/ 251215Z MAR 86
THOMPSON, R.L.	05	000000000	HHC, 3D BN 6 INF/US	ACUTE MYO-CARDIAL INFARCTION	28TH FLD/ 251535Z MAR 86

BRAVO (EXPIRED)

NAME	GRADE	SSN	UNIT/NATION	CAUSE OF DEATH	DTG
WILLIAM, W.R.	E3	000000000	B TRP RECON SQDN/US	BURN, THERMO, 3D DEGREE 18 PERCENT	251415Z MAR 86
MAGSAYSAY, M.			EPW	FRAGMENTATION WOUND OF HEAD	251600Z MAR 86
COMRAD, W.F.	E5	000000000	6 PANZER/GE	RADIATION BURN/MULTIPLE GSWs-SEVERE TRAUMA	251805Z MAR 86

NOTES:

1. THIS IS A BY-NAME REPORT WHICH INCLUDES TWO CATEGORIES OF INFORMATION: THE NAME, GRADE, SSN, UNIT, DIAGNOSIS, AND DESTINATION AND DATE-TIME GROUP OF PATIENTS EVACUATED (ALPHA); AND THE NAME, GRADE, SSN, UNIT AND CAUSE OF DEATH OF PATIENTS WHO EITHER DIED EN ROUTE, OR WHILE AT A REPORTING MTF (BRAVO).

2. THIS REPORT, WHEN COMPLETED, WILL BE CLASSIFIED IN ACCORDANCE WITH LOCAL COMMAND POLICY— ENCODE/ENCRYPT FOR TRANSMISSION.

*UNIT/NATION FOR ENEMY PRISONER OF WAR WILL BE LISTED AS "EPW."

APPENDIX 6

**SAMPLE FORMAT (PATIENT SUMMARY REPORT)
TO ANNEX T, MEDICAL REPORTS**

_____ **INF DIV TSOP**

PATIENT SUMMARY REPORT

DATE-TIME GROUP (DTG): _____

(FROM) / (TO)

		WIA	NBI	DISEASE	*NP	TOTAL
	PATIENTS					
ALPHA	US	_____	_____	_____	_____	_____
BRAVO	ALLIED	_____	_____	_____	_____	_____
CHARLIE	EPW	_____	_____	_____	_____	_____
	DISPOSITION TOTALS					
DELTA	RETURNED TO DUTY			_____		
ECHO	EVACUATED BY AIR			_____		
FOXTROT	EVACUATED BY GROUND			_____		
GOLF	EXPIRED EN ROUTE			_____		
HOTEL	EXPIRED IN MTF			_____		

NOTE: THIS REPORT, WHEN COMPLETED, WILL BE CLASSIFIED IN ACCORDANCE WITH LOCAL COMMAND POLICY—ENCODE/ENCRYPT FOR TRANSMISSION.

*NEUROPSYCHIATRIC STRESS-RELATED PATIENTS SHOULD BE RECORDED HERE.

APPENDIX 7

SAMPLE FORMAT (BLOOD REPORT)
TO ANNEX T, MEDICAL REPORTS

SAMPLE FORMAT A, BLOOD REPORT

_____ INF DIV TSOP

Sample Format A
Message Blood Report

FM: CDR CHARLIE MED 34FSB
TO: BLOOD SUPPORT DETACHMENT OFFICE
INFO: DIVISION SURGEON
CLAS UNCLAS
OPER/VALIANT EAGLE
MSGID/BLDREP/CMED34FSB/1012221//
REF/A/CDRUSACOM/090300ZJAN92/-/TOTAL//
ASOFDTG/100001ZJAN92//   (Line 1)
REPUNIT/CMED34FSB/G/BZ44327432//   (Line 2)
BLDINVT-/-/20JS//   (Line 3)
BLDREQ/30JSW//   (Line 4)
BLDEXP/2JS//   (Line 5)
BLDEST/30JS//   (Line 6)
RMKS/RECEIVED 30JS/TRANSFUSED 30JS/SHIPPED O/   (Line 7)
REFRIGERATOR NEEDS REPAIR//
DECLAS   (Line 8)

*Report Explanation:
(1)   Line 1, ASOFDTG: Day-time zone of the BLDREP.
(2)   Line 2, REPUNIT: Name, designator code, and activity brevity code of reporting unit.
(3)   Line 3, BLDINVT: Used to report the total number of each blood product on hand at the end of the reporting period. Total the blood products at the end of the reporting period.
(4)   Line 4, BLDREQ: Used to report the total number of each blood product requested and time frame needed.
(5)   Line 5, BLDEXP: Used to report the estimate of the number of each blood product which will expire within the next seven days.
(6)   Line 6, BLDEST: Used to report the estimate of the total number of each blood product required for resupply within the next 7 days.
(7)   Line 7, CLOSTEXT OR RMKS: Used to provide additional amplifying information if required.
(8)   Line 8, DECL: Mandatory if the message is classified.

APPENDIX 7 (CONTINUED)

SAMPLE FORMAT (BLOOD REPORT)
TO ANNEX T, MEDICAL REPORTS

SAMPLE FORMAT B, BLOOD REPORT

_____ INF DIV TSOP

Sample Format B
Voice Transmitted Blood Report

LINE 1	151215Z
LINE 2	CHARLIE MIKE 34 HOTEL
LINE 3	20 JS
LINE 4	32 JSW
LINE 5	2 JS
LINE 6	140 JS
LINE 7	RECEIVED 30 JS/ TRANS 20 JS NO UNITS SHIPPED, REFRIGERATOR NEEDS REPAIR
LINE 8	(AUTHENTICATION IN ACCORDANCE WITH SOI)

*Report Explanation

(1)   Line 1, ASOFDTG: Day-time zone of the BLDREP.

(2)   Line 2, REPUNIT: Name, designator code, and activity brevity code of reporting unit.

(3)   Line 3, BLDINVT: Used to report the total number of each blood product on hand at the end of the reporting period. Total the blood products at the end of the reporting period.

(4)   Line 4, BLDREQ: Used to report the total number of each blood product requested and time frame needed.

(5)   Line 5, BLDEXP: Used to report the estimate of the number of each blood product which will expire within the next seven days.

(6)   Line 6, BLDEST: Used to report the estimate of the total number of each blood product required for resupply within the next 7 days.

(7)   Line 7, CLOSTEXT OR RMKS: Used to provide additional amplifying information if required.

(8)   Line 8, AUTHENTICATE: Authentication, if required.

APPENDIX 8

**SAMPLE FORMAT (TEAM MOVEMENT REPORT)
TO ANNEX T, MEDICAL REPORTS**

_____ INF DIV TSOP

FM: FSMC
TO: SUPPORT OPERATIONS FSB//BRIGADE SURGEON'S SEC//DIVISION SURGEON'S SECTION

INFORMATION: NONE

CLASSIFICATION: AS APPROPRIATE

SUBJECT: TEAM MOVEMENT REPORT

LINE ONE: UNIT WILL BE REPORTED AS ALPHA, BRAVO, CHARLIE, ETC

LINE TWO: CURRENT LOCATION, SIX DIGIT GRID COORDINATES

LINE THREE: DEPARTURE AS OF: (DTG IN ZULU TIME)

LINE FOUR: DESTINATION AND ROUTE

LINE FIVE: ARRIVAL AS OF: (DTG IN ZULU TIME)

                          LINES TWO THROUGH FOUR ARE REPORTED PRIOR TO DEPARTURE FROM
                          ANY SITE; LINE FIVE IS REPORTED UPON ARRIVAL

APPENDIX 9

SAMPLE FORMAT (REPORTS CODES)
TO ANNEX T, MEDICAL REPORTS

_____ INF DIV TSOP

1.   PURPOSE: To list medical codes used to assist medical units in filling out medical reports and Class VIII resupply requests.

2.   FREQUENCY: NA.

3.   RESPONSIBILITY: Division surgeon.

4.   ADDRESSEES: All medical units.

5.   TRANSMISSION: NA.

6.   REPORTS FORMAT: NA.

7.   REMARKS:

A.   Each major command (MACOM) establishes reporting codes which meet operational requirements for their units.

B.   The following tables (TABs) will assist in compiling the report as required.

(1)   TAB A: Table of Minimum Essential Supply Items

(2)   TAB B: Disease Codes

(3)   TAB C: Authorized Abbreviations

(4)   TAB D: Cause of Casualty

TAB A (TABLE OF MINIMUM ESSENTIAL SUPPLY ITEMS) TO APPENDIX 9 (REPORT CODES) TO ANNEX T, MEDICAL REPORTS

_____INF DIV TSOP

SURGICAL DRESSING MATERIEL

090	BANDAGE, GAUZE ROLLER
091	FIRST AID DRESSING
092	BURN DRESSING
093	GAUZE, ABSORBENT
094	BANDAGE, COTTON PLASTER OF PARIS, IMPREGNATED
095	COTTON WOOL, ABSORBENT

GASTROINTESTINAL

100	ANTIHELMINTIC
101	ANTIDIARRHEAL
102	ANTIDYSENTERIC
103	ANTACIDS

MISCELLANEOUS

110	DISINFECTANTS
111	ANTISEPTICS
112	DETERGENTS, SURGICAL
113	HYPODERMIC SYRINGES AND NEEDLES
114	SURGICAL SUTURE/LIGATURE MATERIEL
115	SPLINTING MATERIEL

TAB B (DISEASE CODES) TO APPENDIX 9 (REPORT CODES)
TO ANNEX T, MEDICAL REPORTS

_____INF DIV TSOP

DISEASE	CODE
Cholera	000
Typhoid Fever	001
Paratyphoid Fever	002
Other Salmonella Infections	003
Bacillary Dysentery	004
Amoebiasis	006
Other Enteric Infection	008
Pulmonary Tuberculosis	010
Plague	020
Tularemia	021
Anthrax	022
Brucellosis	023
Dyptheria	032
Scarlet Fever	034
Erysipelas	035
Meningococcal Infection	036
Tetanus	037
Acute Poliomyelitis	043
Smallpox	050
Chicken Pox	052
Measles	055
Rubeola	056
Yellow Fever	060
Viral Encephalitis (unspecified)	065
Infectious Hepatitis	070
Epidemic Parotitis	072
Mononucleosis	075
Epidemic Louse-Borne Typhus	080
Q-Fever	083
Malaria	084
Relapsing Fever	088
Syphilis	090
Blennorrhea	098
Venereal Ulcers	099
Leptospirosis	100
Influenza	470
Other	989 (If this code is used, provide details.)

**TAB C (AUTHORIZED ABBREVIATIONS) TO APPENDIX 9 (REPORT CODES)
TO ANNEX T, MEDICAL REPORTS**

_____INF DIV TSOP

AUTHORIZED ABBREVIATIONS

ARMS AND SERVICES:

AVN	AVIATION	EMPLOYED MEANS:
ABN	AIRBORNE	MORTARS
AD	AIR DEFENSE	POISON
AMINF	ARMED INFANTRY	ROCKETS
AMPB	AMPHIBIOUS	SABOTAGE
ARMD	ARMORED	TUBEARTY
ARTY	ARTILLERY	MISSILES
AT	ANTITANK	
ATAGM	ANTITANK GUIDED MISSILE	

COMMAND LEVEL:

AG	ADJUTANT GENERAL
ARMY	ARMY
BDE	BRIGADE
BN	BATTALION
CO	COMPANY
CORPS	CORPS
DIV	DIVISION
GP	GROUP
HQ	HEADQUARTERS
PLT	PLATOON
RGT	REGIMENT

NATIONALITY:

BE	BELGIAN
CA	CANADIAN
GE	GERMAN
NL	NETHERLANDS/HOLLAND
UK	BRITISH
US	AMERICAN

TAB D (CAUSE OF CASUALTY) TO APPENDIX 9 (REPORT CODES) TO ANNEX T, MEDICAL REPORTS

_____INF DIV TSOP

CAUSE OF CASUALTY TO BE USED FOR MASS CASUALTY REPORTING.

ACCIDENT:	AIRCRASH
ACCIDENT:	MARITIME
ACCIDENT:	MOTOR VEHICLE
ACCIDENT:	RAILWAY
ACCIDENT:	FIRE
ACCIDENT:	INDUSTRIAL
ACCIDENT:	POISON
ACCIDENT:	NATURAL DISASTERS
ACCIDENT:	OTHER CAUSES
BATTLE:	CONVENTIONAL
BATTLE:	NUCLEAR
BATTLE:	BIOLOGICAL
BATTLE:	CHEMICAL

APPENDIX C

BRIGADE SURGEON'S SECTION INITIAL BRIGADE COMBAT TEAM

C-1. Mission of the Brigade Surgeon's Section

The mission of the BSS is to plan, coordinate, and synchronize CHS for the brigade. This is accomplished under the supervision of the brigade surgeon. The BSS looks at the total CHS package in support of the brigade and plans its employment to ensure maximum coverage and effective utilization of brigade medical personnel. For definitive information on developing CHS input for the OPLAN/OPORD, see FMs 8-55, 101-5, and 101-5-1.

C-2. Brigade Surgeon's Section

a. The BSS (Figure C-1) is assigned to the HHC of the brigade and operates out of the brigade TOC. The BSS is an integral part of the brigade's main CP and the staff of the BSS is intimately involved with the S3 and his staff in the planning process. A surgeon's cell and a medical plans and operations cell form the BSS. This section, in coordination with the HSSO and HSMO of the brigade support battalion (BSB) support operations section, and the brigade support medical company (BSMC) commander, is responsible for the development of the medical portion of the brigade OPLAN/OPORD and takes part in the brigade planning process. The BSS staff is responsible to the brigade commander for staff supervision of CHS within the brigade. The BSS is also responsible for coordinating GS and DS relationships of organic medical units and other medical units/elements whether under OPCON or attached to the brigade. The brigade commander is updated as required on the status of CHS in the brigade.

b. The brigade surgeon is the chief of the BSS and is assisted by the medical plans and operations cell. Specific functions of the BSS include—

- Planning and ensuring that Echelons I and II CHS for the brigade are provided in a timely and efficient manner.

- Planning and coordinating CHS operations for brigade medical assets and attached or OPCON corps assets. This includes reinforcement and reconstitution.

- Coordinating with the FSB support operations CHS cell HSSO and HSMO for prioritizing the reallocation of organic and corps medical augmentation assets as required by the tactical situation.

- Ensuring that the medical annex of the brigade TSOPs, plans, policies, and procedures for CHS, prescribed by the brigade surgeon, are prepared and executed.

- Overseeing medical training (collective and individual) and providing information to the brigade surgeon and brigade commander.

- Coordinating and prioritizing CHL and blood management requirements for the brigade.

• Collecting medical threat information and coordinating combat health intelligence requirements with the brigade S2 according to FM 8-10-8.

• Coordinating and directing patient evacuation from the brigade AO to supporting MTFs.

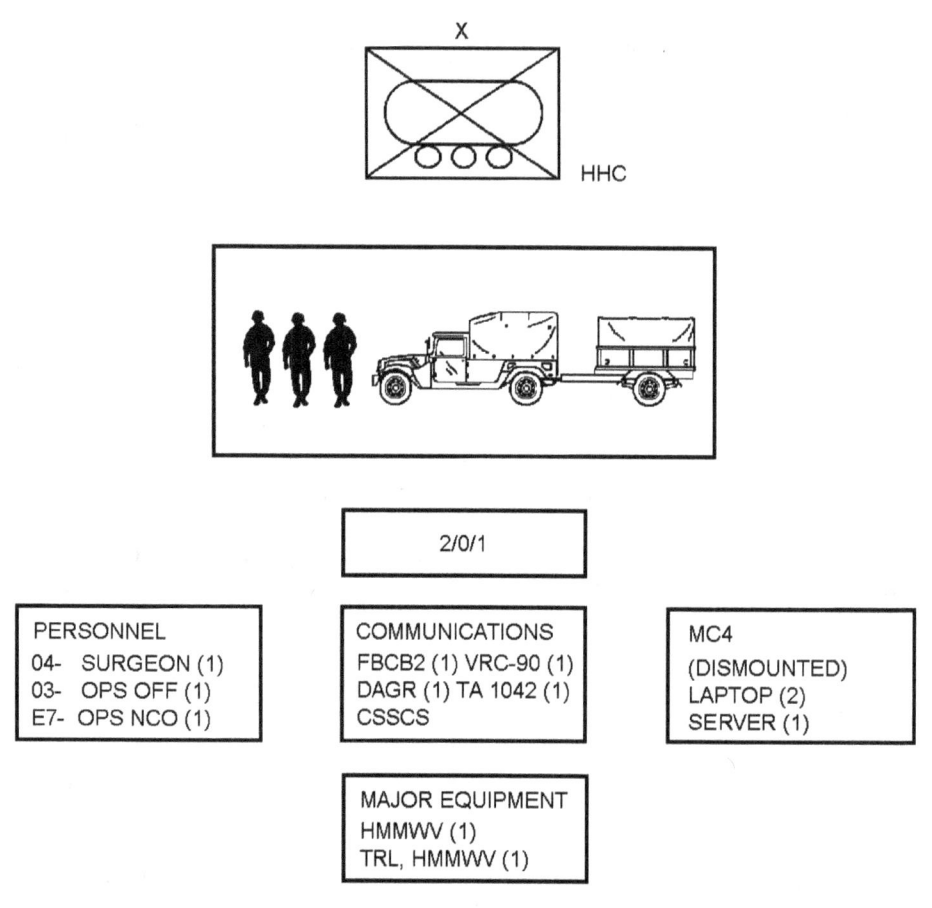

Figure C-1. Brigade surgeon's section.

• Coordinating the medical evacuation of all EPW casualties from the brigade AO.

• Coordinating the disposition of captured medical materiel.

• Coordinating, planning, and prioritizing PVNTMED missions.

• Coordinating with the supporting veterinary element for subsistence and animal disease surveillance.

- Coordinating medical intelligence preparation of the battlefield.

- Advising on the ramification of using nonlethal weapons and how this might affect the CHS plan.

C-3. Duties and Responsibilities of the Brigade Surgeon

The brigade surgeon is an MC officer (Major, AOC 62B00). He is a special staff officer who plans with and coordinates brigade CHS activities with the brigade S1. The surgeon is responsible for the technical control of all medical activities in the command. The brigade surgeon oversees and coordinates CHS activities through the BSS and the brigade S3. The brigade surgeon keeps the brigade commander informed on the status of CHS for brigade operations and the health of the command. He provides input and obtains information to facilitate medical planning. For definitive information pertaining to the brigade surgeon's duties and responsibilities, see FM 8-10-21.

C-4. Medical Plans and Operations Cell

The medical plans and operations cell is typically staffed with a—

- Medical plans officer (Captain, AOC 70H67).

- Medical operations NCO (E-7, MOS 91B40).

This cell is responsible for—

- Developing CHS staff estimates for supporting brigade operations.

- Developing and coordinating the brigade CHS plan with the brigade staff, the BSB staff, the BSMC, and the maneuver battalion medical platoons.

- Developing the CHS annex of the brigade OPLAN/OPORD.

- Overseeing and synchronizing brigade CHS operations.

- Monitoring medical troop strength to determine task organization for mission accomplishment.

- Forwarding all medical information of potential intelligence value to the brigade S2 and S3 sections.

- Obtaining updated medical threat and intelligence information through the brigade S2 and S3 sections and from the higher headquarters for evaluation and applicability.

• Coordinating the disposition of captured medical materiels according to the TSOPs.

• Coordinating through the higher headquarters for corps-level medical support reinforcement/augmentation, as required.

• Verifying emergency supply requests and taking the necessary action to expedite delivery.

• Monitoring Class VIII resupply levels to ensure adequate stockage for support of brigade operations.

• Tracking and managing critical Class VIII items in coordination with the maneuver battalion medical platoons and the BSMC.

• Ensuring that clear and accurate patient records are maintained of all clinical encounters for supported deployed personnel through the use of a DA Form 8007-R or through the use of digital patient records, as they become available. See AR 40-66 and FM 8-10-1 for management of individual health records in the field. Also, digital patient records at the division and brigade level will be available through the fielding of MC4 and the TMIP.

C-5. Information and Communications

a. *The Brigade Surgeon's Section's Communications and Information Systems.* Information and communications assets available to the BSS include radio sets (AN/VRC 90 series [FM]); digital nonsecure voice telephone (1 each); MSE FAX; TACLAN WS; LAN router; MCS; CSSCS; and FBCB2/position/navigation (1 each). The CSSCS in the BSS will aid with maintaining real-time situational awareness and with understanding what is happening on the battlefield. This system tracks unit information down to the company level. Included in the classes of supplies tracked by the CSSCS is Class VIII. Using the CSSCS to track Class VIII will enhance the BSS's ability to identify critical Class VIII items. The BSS will exchange information with the FSB and higher headquarters, using the CSSCS. For definitive information on the CSSCS, see FMs 63-20-1, 63-21-1, and 63-23-2.

b. *Combat Health Support Functions, Force XXI Battle Command Brigade and Below System.* Force XXI Battle Command Brigade and Below is a hardware/software suite that digitizes C2 at brigade and below level. The FBCB2 system provides a seamless battle command capability for performance of missions throughout the operational continuum at the tactical level. The FBCB2 system is the implementation of information technology to provide increased battlefield operational capabilities. The system is positioned on specified platforms and will perform combat, CS, and CSS functions for the planning and execution of operations. This system gives the BSS a common relevant picture of the current CHS situation at BAS, AXPs, and the BSMC. For the first time, the medical organizations and elements are digitally linked to the platforms and organizations they support, providing current information on the status of those units. This common battlefield picture will enable CHS providers to maintain the operational tempo set by the maneuver commander. There are three medical screens incorporated into the CSS FBCB2 function. They are the medical functionality in the LOGSITREP, the MEDSITREP, and the MEDEVAC request. It is important that units use standard message and report formats to eliminate confusion.

c. *Radio Nets.* Radio nets used by the BSS includes the following:

(1) The BSS maintains communication with medical elements supporting the brigade through its FM radio. Single-channel ground and airborne radio system components provide the BSS with an AN/VRC 90. A technique for operating a brigade medical net is to use the BSMC command net for brigade-wide medical communications while using the administrative/logistics net for other CSS integration. Situation awareness is monitored using FBCB2 and by face-to-face contact with other brigade staff members in the brigade TOC.

(2) The brigade logistics operations net (AM-SSB), which is controlled by the BSB support operations section, provides the necessary long-range C2 link between the FSB, the brigade, and supporting corps logistics elements.

d. *Mobile Subscriber Equipment.* Mobile subscriber equipment allows the BSS to communicate throughout the battlefield in either a mobile or static situation. As the Army continues to digitize the battlefield and modernize the force, the use of automation continues to develop. Mobile subscriber equipment packet switching network gives units the ability to connect to division and corps LANs or WAN. A WAN is similar to the LAN but covers a larger distance. This allows units/CPs to connect computer systems, such as the CSSCS, MCS, and FBCB2, to an ethernet cable (coaxial) and send and receive information in an extremely efficient manner. Because of the limitations of a network constructed with coaxial cable, a WAN uses a combination of the MSE packet network and radio networks to distribute the data through the system where necessary. Packet switching does not use or take up existing telephone lines. Instead, telephone lines are freed up even more because information is being sent over a network on computers and related equipment. Using the ATCCS, common hardware/software facilitates the interface and exchange of information between the BSS, medical platoons operating BAS, BSMC, and corps medical elements. See FM 63-2-2 for information concerning ADP continuity of the operations plan.

e. *Combat Service Support Control System.* The CSSCS is the CSS component of ABCS. This is the primary CSS information tool used within the brigade. The CSSCS provides a concise picture of unit requirements and support capabilities by collecting, processing, and displaying information on key items of supplies, services, and personnel that the commanders deem crucial to the success of an operation. The CSSCS currently provides situation awareness of critical elements within supply Classes I, II/IV, IIIB, IIIP, V, VII, and VIII and personnel strength management. Maintenance, transportation, and medical functionality are a few features to be added as the system matures.

C-6. Medical Standard Army Management Information System

The MC4 system will be a theater, automated CHS system, which links commanders, health care providers, and supporting elements, at all echelons, with integrated medical information. The BSS has one MC4 system (dismounted) with two laptops and one server. The system provides digital enablers to connect both vertically and horizontally, all ten CHS functional business systems. See Chapter 2 for definitive information on MC4.

C-7. Brigade Combat Health Support Planning

The brigade plan/operations cell has the primary responsibility for developing and coordinating the brigade's CHS plan. The foundation of the brigade's CHS plan is the brigade commander's guidance and the higher headquarters' CHS plan. The BSS is an integral member of the planning staff and participates in all phases of the tactical decision making process. For definitive information on planning and conducting CHS operations for the digitized force, see FM 8-10-21.

C-8. Combat Health Support Tactical Standing Operating Procedures

The BSS is responsible for the development of the CHS annex for the brigade TSOPs. The purpose of a TSOP is to establish routine protocols. The procedures in the TSOP should not be dependent upon the METT-TC factors. If a specific decision is required each time, it should not be included in the TSOP. The brigade's TSOP is based on its higher headquarters' TSOP and serves as the foundation for subordinate units to develop their TSOP. The brigade's CHS annexes to the TSOP should be clear and concise, yet provide sufficient detail of procedural requirements. The CHS annexes to the TSOP must reflect procedural guidance that supports current mission and doctrinal requirements. The CHS annexes to the brigade's TSOP should be maintained and reviewed at least every 6 months and revised as required. Most importantly the TSOP must be trained and understood at all levels prior to deployment or it has no real value.

GLOSSARY

ABBREVIATIONS, ACRONYMS, AND DEFINITIONS

A2C2   Army airspace command and control

ABCA   American, British, Canadian, and Australian

ABCS   Army Battle Command System

ACM   airspace control measures

ACUS   area common-user system

ADCS   assistant division commander for support

ADP   automatic data processing

AEV   armored evacuation vehicle

AFATDS   Advanced Field Artillery Tactical Data System

AM   amplitude modulated

AMDWS   air missile defense workstations

AMEDD   Army Medical Department

AMEDDC&S   Army Medical Department Center and School

AO   area of operations

AOC   area of concentration

AR   Army regulation

Armed Services Whole Blood Processing Laboratories (ASWBPL)   Triservice operated facilities located at United States Air Force airheads in continental United States that receive blood from continental United States-based blood donor centers. Its functions include replacing blood from the blood donor centers, storing blood, and distributing blood to Blood Transshipment Centers located in the communications zone.

ASMB   area support medical battalion

ASOFDTG   as of date-time group

ASWBPL   *See* Armed Services Whole Blood Processing Laboratories.

ATCCS   Army Tactical Command and Control System

ATM   advanced trauma management

attn   attention

augmentation   The addition of specialized personnel and/or equipment to a unit.

authorized stockage list   A list of items from **all** classes of supply authorized to be stocked at a specific echelon of supply.

AVIM   aviation intermediate maintenance

AXP   ambulance exchange point

BAS   battalion aid station

basic load   For other than ammunition, basic loads are supplies kept by using units in combat. The quantity of each item of supply in a basic load is related to the number of days in combat the unit may be sustained without resupply.

BCT   brigade combat team

BD   battlefield distribution

bde   brigade

BF   battle fatigue

BLDEST   blood estimate

BLDEXP   blood expired

BLDINVT   blood inventory

BLDREP   blood report

BLDREQ   blood request

boundary   A control measure normally drawn along identifiable terrain features and used to delineate areas of tactical responsibility for subordinate units. Within their boundaries, units may maneuver within the overall plan without close coordination with neighboring units unless otherwise restricted. Direct fire may be placed across boundaries on clearly identified enemy targets without prior

coordination, provided friendly forces are not endangered. Indirect fire also may be used after prior coordination.
Lateral boundaries are used to control combat operations of adjacent units.
Rear boundaries are established to facilitate command and control.

br   branch

brigade support area (BSA)   A designated area in which combat service support elements from the division support command and the corps support command provide logistic support to a brigade. The brigade support area normally is located 20 to 25 kilometers behind the forward edge of the battle area.

BRIL   baseline resource item list

BSA   *See* brigade support area.

BSB   brigade support battalion

BSMC   brigade support medical company

BSS   brigade surgeon's section(s)

BSU   blood supply unit

C2   *See* command and control.

camouflage   The use of concealment and disguise to minimize detection or identification of troops, weapons, equipment, and installations. It includes taking advantage of the immediate environment as well as using natural and artificial materials.

casualty   Any person who is lost to his organization by reason of having been declared dead, wounded, injured, diseased, interned, captured, retained, missing in action, beleaguered, besieged, or detained.

cbt   combat

CDR   commander

chain of command   The succession of commanding officers from a superior to a subordinate through which command is exercised.

CHL   combat health logistics

CHS   *See* combat health support.

CIP combat identification panel

cl class

CLAS classified

CMCC corps movement control center

co company

COA course(s) of action

coll collecting/collection

combat health support (CHS) All support services performed, provided, or arranged by the Army Medical Department to promote, improve, conserve, or restore the mental and/or physical well-being of personnel in the Army and, as directed, in other services, agencies, and organizations. These services include, but are not limited to, the management of health service resources such as manpower, monies, and facilities; preventive and curative health measures; the health service doctrine; evacuation of the sick (physically and mentally), injured, and wounded; selection of the medically fit and disposition of the medically unfit; medical supply, equipment, and maintenance thereof; and medical, dental, veterinary, laboratory, optometry, and medical food services.

combat intelligence That knowledge of the enemy, weather, and geographical features required by a commander in planning and conducting combat operations. It is derived from the analysis of information on the enemy's capabilities, intentions, and vulnerabilities and the environment.

combat maneuver forces Those forces which use fire and movement to engage the enemy with direct fire weapon systems, as distinguished from those forces which engage the enemy with indirect fires or otherwise provide combat support. These elements are primarily infantry, armor, cavalry (air and armored), and aviation.

combat medic A medical specialist, trained in emergency medical treatment procedures, and assigned or attached in support of a combat or combat support unit.

combat service support (CSS) The support provided to sustain combat forces, primarily in the fields of administration and logistics. It may include administrative service, chaplain service, civil affairs, food service, finance, legal service, maintenance, medical service, military police, supply, transportation, and other logistical services. The basic mission of combat service support is to develop and maintain maximum combat power through the support of weapons systems.

combat support (CS) Fire support and operational assistance provided to combat elements. May include artillery, air defense, aviation (less air cavalry and attack helicopter), engineer, military police, signal, and electronic warfare.

combat trains   The portion of unit trains that provides the combat service support required for immediate response to the needs of forward tactical elements.   At company level, medical, recovery, and maintenance elements normally constitute the combat trains.   At battalion, the combat trains normally consist of ammunition and petroleum, oil and lubricants vehicles, maintenance/recovery vehicles and crews, and the battalion aid station.

command and control (C2)   The exercise of command that is the process through which the activities of military forces are directed, coordinated, and controlled to accomplish the mission.   This process encompasses the personnel, equipment, communications, facilities, and procedures necessary to gather and analyze information, to plan for what is to be done, and to supervise the execution of operations.

command post (CP)   The principal facility employed by the commander to command and control combat operations.   A command post consists of those coordinating and special staff activities and representatives from supporting Army elements and other services that may be necessary to carry out operations.   Corps and division headquarters are particularly adaptable to organization by echelon into a tactical command post, a main command post, and a rear command post.

commander's estimate   The procedure whereby a commander decides how best to accomplish the assigned mission.   It is a thorough consideration of the mission, enemy, terrain, troops available, time, and other relevant factors.   The commander's estimate is based on personal knowledge of the situation and on staff estimates.

commander's intent   Commander's vision of the battle—how he expects to fight and what he expects to accomplish.

concealment   The protection from observation.

concept of operations   A graphic, verbal, or written statement in broad outline that gives an overall picture of a commander's assumptions or intent in regard to an operation or series of operations; includes at a minimum the scheme of maneuver and the fire support plan.   The concept of operations is embodied in campaign plans and operation plans particularly when the plans cover a series of connected operations to be carried out simultaneously or in succession.   It is described in sufficient detail for the staff and subordinate commanders to understand what they are to do and how to fight the battle without further instructions.

CONUS   continental United States

COTS   commercial off-the-shelf

CP   *See* command post.

CS   *See* combat support.

CSC   combat stress control

CSH   combat support hospital

CSS *See* combat service support.

CSSCS Combat Service Support Control System

CTCP combat trains combat post

CTIL commander's tracked item(s) list

DA Department of the Army

DAGR defense advanced GPS receiver

DASB division aviation support battalion

DDL daily disposition log

DECL declassified

direct support (DS) (1) A mission requiring a force to support another specific force and authorizing it to answer directly the supported force's request for assistance. (2) In the North Atlantic Treaty Organization, the support provided by a unit or formation not attached to, nor under command of, the supported unit or formation, but required to give priority to the support required by that unit or formation.

DISCOM division support command

disp disposition

div division

division support area (DSA) An area normally located in the division rear positioned near air landing facilities and along the main supply route.

DMC distribution management center

DMLSS Defense Medical Logistics Standard Support

DMMC division materiel management center

DNBI disease and nonbattle injury

DOD Department of Defense

DS *See* direct support.

DSA *See* division support area.

DSB division support battalion

DSMC division support medical company

DSS division surgeon's section

DTG date-time group

DTO division transportation office

DVE driver's vision enhancer

E-mail electronic mail

EAD echelons above division

Echelon I (Level I) Unit level—The first medical care a soldier receives is provided at this level. This care includes immediate lifesaving measures, advanced trauma management, disease prevention, combat stress control prevention, casualty collection, and evacuation from supported unit to supporting medical treatment. Echelon I elements are located throughout the combat and communications zones. These elements include the combat lifesaver, combat medic, and battalion aid station. Some or all of these elements are found in maneuver, combat support, and combat service support units. When Echelon I is not present in a unit, this support is provided to that unit by Echelon II medical units.

Echelon II (Level II) Duplicates Echelon I and expands services available by adding dental, laboratory, x-ray, and patient holding capabilities. Emergency care, advanced trauma management, including beginning resuscitation procedures, is continued. (No general anesthesia is available.) If necessary, additional emergency measures are instituted; however, they do not go beyond the measures dictated by the immediate needs. Echelon II units are located in the combat zone—brigade support area, corps support area, and communications zone. Echelon II medical support may be provided by a clearing station, forward support medical company, main support medical company, forward support battalion medical company, main support battalion medical company, corps area medical companies, area support medical company (Medical Force 2000), and communications zone medical companies.

Echelon III (Level III) This echelon of support expands the support provided at Echelon II (division level). Casualties who are unable to tolerate and survive movement over long distances will receive surgical care in hospitals as close to the division rear boundary as the tactical situation will allow. This may be provided within the division area under certain operational conditions. Echelon III characterizes the care that is provided by units such as the mobile army surgical hospital, the combat support hospital, and the evacuation hospital. Operational conditions may require Echelon III units to locate in offshore support facilities, third country support bases, or in the communications zone.

Echelon IV (Level IV)   This echelon of care is provided in a general hospital and in other communications zone-level facilities which are staffed and equipped for general and specialized medical and surgical treatment. This echelon of care provides further treatment to stabilize those patients requiring evacuation to continental United States. This echelon also provides area combat health support to soldiers within the communications zone.

Echelon of Care   A North Atlantic Treaty Organization term which can be used interchangeably with the term *level of care*.

emergency medical treatment (EMT)   The immediate application of medical procedures to the wounded, injured, or sick by specially trained medical personnel.

EMT   *See* emergency medical treatment.

EPLRS   Enhanced Position Location Reporting System

EPW   enemy prisoner(s) of war

ETA   estimated time of arrival

evac   *See* evacuation.

evacuation (evac)   (1) A combat service support function which involves the movement of recovered materiel from a main supply route, maintenance collecting point, and maintenance activity to higher levels of maintenance. (2) The process of moving any person who is wounded, injured, or ill to and/or between medical treatment facilities.

evacuation policy   A command decision indicating the length in days of the maximum period of non-effectiveness that patients may be held within the command for treatment. Patients who, in the opinion of an officiating medical officer, cannot be returned to duty status within the period prescribed are evacuated by the first available means, provided the travel involved will not aggravate their disabilities.

fax   facsimile

FBCB2   *See* Force XXI Battle Command Brigade and Below System.

1SG   first sergeant

FLOT   forward line of own troops

FM   field manual (when used with a number), frequency modulated

FMC   US Field Medical Card

FMS   Force XXI manning system

Force XXI Battle Command Brigade and Below (FBCB2)   This is a digital, battle command information system that provides mounted/dismounted tactical combat, combat support, and combat service support commanders, leaders, and soldiers integrated, on-the-move, real-time/near real-time, battle command information and situational awareness from brigade down to the soldier/platform level across all battlefield functional areas. The FBCB2 is located in the mounted and dismounted maneuver (divisional, separate, heavy, and light) armor/cavalry/reconnaissance, and armored cavalry, mechanized infantry, infantry, and aviation units.

FSB   forward support battalion

FSC   forward support company

FSMC   forward support medical company

FSMT   forward support MEDEVAC team

FST   forward surgical team

G1   Assistant Chief of Staff (Personnel)

G2   Assistant Chief of Staff (Intelligence)

G3   Assistant Chief of Staff (Operations and Plans)

G4   Assistant Chief of Staff (Logistics)

G5   Assistant Chief of Staff (Civil Affairs)

G6   Assistant Chief of Staff (Signal)

GCCS-A   Global Command and Control System-Army

general support (GS)   Support that is given to the supported force as a whole and not to any particular subdivision thereof.

GOTS   government off-the-shelf

GPS   global positioning system

GS   *See* general support.

GSO   general supply office

GTN   Global Traffic Network

HHC   headquarters and headquarters company

HMMWV   high mobility multipurpose wheeled vehicle

HN   host nation

HSMO   health service materiel officer

HSSO   health service support officer

I/R   Internment/Resettlement

ID   identification

IHFR   improved high-frequency radio

inf   infantry

information requirements   Those items of information regarding the enemy and his environment which need to be collected and processed in order to meet the intelligence requirements of a commander.

intel   *See* intelligence.

intelligence (intel)   The product resulting from the collection, evaluation, analysis, integration, and interpretation of all available information concerning an enemy force, foreign nations, or areas of operations, and which is immediately or potentially significant to military planning and operations.

intelligence preparation of the battlefield   A systematic approach to analyzing the enemy, weather, and terrain in a specific geographic area. It integrates enemy doctrine with the weather and terrain as they relate to the mission, and the specific battlefield environment. This is done to determine and evaluate enemy capabilities, vulnerabilities, and probable courses of action.

IPB   intelligence preparation of the battlefield

ISB   intermediate staging base

KP   kitchen police

LAN local area network

LD line of departure

lines of communication (LOC) All the routes (land, water, and air) that connect an operating military force with one or more bases of operations, and along which supplies and military forces move.

LOC *See* lines of communication.

local security Those security elements established in the proximity of a unit to prevent surprise by the enemy.

logistics The planning and carrying out of the movement and the maintenance of forces. In its most comprehensive sense, those aspects of military operations which deal with—(1) design and development, acquisition, storage, movement, maintenance, and distribution of material; (2) movement, evacuation, and hospitalization of personnel; (3) acquisition or construction, maintenance, operation, and disposition of facilities; and (4) acquisition or furnishing of services.

LOGPAC logistical package

LOGSITREP logistics situation report

LTC lieutenant colonel

LZ landing zone

MACOM major command

maint maintenance

MAT materiel

MC Medical Corps

MC4 Medical Communications for Combat Casualty Care

MCO movement control office(r)

MCS maneuver control system

MDMP military decision-making process

MDT medical detachment-telemedicine

med/MED medical

MEDCOM medical command

MEDEVAC medical evacuation

medical equipment set(s) (MES) A chest containing medical instruments and supplies designed for specific table of organization and equipment units or missions.

medical intelligence A functional area of technical intelligence resulting from the collection, evaluation, analysis, and interpretation of foreign medical, biotechnological, and environmental information.

medical treatment facility (MTF) Any facility established for the purpose of providing medical treatment. This includes aid stations, clearing stations, dispensaries, clinics, and hospitals.

MEDLOG medical logistics

MEDLOG-D medical logistics-division

MEDSITREP medical situation report

MEDSTEP Medical Standby Equipment Program

MES *See* medical equipment set(s).

METT-TC mission, enemy, terrain, troops, time available, and civilian considerations

mgt management

MMMB medical materiel management branch

MOS military occupational specialty(ies)

MPL mandatory parts list

MRO medical regulating office(r)

msg message

MSE mobile subscriber equipment

MSGID message identification

MSRT mobile subscriber radiotelephone

MTF *See* medical treatment facility.

MTOE modification table(s) of organization and equipment

MTS movement tracking system

NA not applicable

NATO North Atlantic Treaty Organization

NBC nuclear, biological, and chemical

NCO noncommissioned officer

NEO noncombatant evacuation operation(s)

NP neuropsychiatric

NRTD nonreturn to duty

NVG night vision goggles

OCOKA observation and fields of fire, concealment and cover, obstacles, key terrain, and avenues of approach

OEG operational exposure guidance

ofc office

off officer

oper operation

OPCON *See* operational control.

operational control (OPCON) The authority delegated to a commander to direct forces assigned so that the commander may accomplish specific missions or tasks that are usually limited by function, time, or location; to deploy units concerned, and to retain or assign tactical control of those units. It does not of itself include administrative or logistic control. In the North Atlantic Treaty Organization, it does not include authority to assign separate employment of components of the units concerned.

operation order (OPORD) A directive issued by a commander to subordinate commanders for effecting the coordinated execution of an operation; includes tactical movement orders.

operation plan (OPLAN) A plan for a military operation. It covers a single operation or series of connected operations to be carried out simultaneously or in succession. It implements operations derived from the campaign plan. When the time and/or conditions under which the plan is to be placed in effect occur, the plan becomes an operation order.

OPLAN *See* operation plan.

OPORD *See* operation order.

ops/OPS operations

OPSEC operations security

PA physician assistant

pam pamphlet

PE&MR Patient Evacuation and Mortality Report

PERSITREP personnel situation report

PIC Personal Information Carrier

PLL prescribed load list

plt platoon

PMCS preventive maintenance checks and services

pnt/PNT patient

POL petroleum, oils and lubricants

PSR Patient Summary Report

PSYOP psychological operations

pub publication

PVNTMED preventive medicine

QSTAG Quadripartite Standardization Agreement

R/T receiver/transmitter

RAU radio access unit

Reconstitution The total process of keeping the force supplied with various supply classes, services, and replacement personnel and equipment required to maintain the desired level of combat effectiveness and of restoring units that are not combat effective to the desired level of combat effectiveness through the replacement of critical equipment and personnel. Reconstitution encompasses unit regeneration and sustaining support.

REPUNIT reporting unit

rpts reports

rtd return(ed) to duty

S1 Adjutant (US Army)

S2 Intelligence Officer (US Army)

S3 Operations and Training Officer (US Army)

S4 Supply Officer (US Army)

S6 Communication Staff Officer (US Army)

SAAFR standard Army aircraft flight routes

SB supply bulletin

sec section

SINCGARS Single-Channel Ground and Airborne Radio System

SIP Systems Improvement Program

SITREP situation report

SOI signal operation instructions

SOP standing operating procedures

spt support

SRC standard requirements code

SSB single sideband

STAMIS Standard Army Management Information System

STANAG Standardization Agreement

sup supply

surg surgeon

TA theater Army

TAB table

TACCS Tactical Army Combat Service Support (CSS) Computer System

TACLAN tactical local area network

TAMMIS Theater Army Medical Management Information System

TB technical bulletin

TCAIMS Transportation Coordinator's Automated Information for Movement System

TM/tm technical manual/team

TMIP Theater Medical Information Program

TOC tactical operations center

TOE table(s) of organization and equipment

trans transportation

trl trailer

trmt treatment

TSOP tactical standing operating procedure(s)

ULC unit-level computer

US   United States

USAF   United States Air Force

USR   unit status reporting

WAN   wide area network

WARNO   warning order

WIA   wounded in action

WIN   warfighter information network

WS   weather system, work station

WX   weather

XO   executive officer

REFERENCES

SOURCES USED

These are the sources quoted or paraphrased in this publication.

NATO STANAGs

These agreements are available on request using DD Form 1425 from Standardization Document Order Desk, 700 Robin Avenue, Building 4, Section D, Philadelphia, Pennsylvania 19111-5094.

2027. *Marking of Military Vehicles.* 18 December 1975. (Latest Amendment, 25 April 1991.)

2874. *Planning Guide for the Estimation of Battle Casualties (Nuclear)—AMedP-8.* 27 November 1981. (Latest Amendment, 26 April 1994.)

2931. *Orders for the Camouflage of the Red Cross and Red Crescent on Land in Tactical Operations (Edition 2).* 19 January 1998. (Latest Amendment, 3 April 1998.)

ABCA QSTAG

This agreement is available on request using DD Form 1425 from the Standardization Document Order Desk, 700 Robins Avenue, Building 4, Section D, Philadelphia, Pennsylvania 19111-5094.

512. *Marking of Military Vehicles.* 31 January 1979. (Latest Amendment, 9 October 1980.)

Joint and Multiservice Publications

Joint Pub 3-07.3. *Joint Tactics, Techniques and Procedures for Peace Operations.* 12 February 1999.

Joint Pub 4-02. *Doctrine for Health Services Support in Joint Operations.* 26 April 1995.

FM 3-3. *Chemical and Biological Contamination Avoidance.* FMFM 11-17. 16 November 1992. (Change 1, 29 September 1994.)

FM 3-3-1. *Nuclear Contamination Avoidance.* FMFM 11-18. 9 September 1994.

FM 8-284 (4-02.284). *Treatment of Biological Warfare Agent Casualties.* NAVMED P-5042; AFMAN(I) 44-156; MCRP 4-11.1C. 17 July 2000.

FM 8-285 (4-02.285). *Treatment of Chemical Agent Casualties and Conventional Military Chemical Injuries.* NAVMED P-5041; AFJMAN 44-149; FMFM 11-11. 22 December 1995.

*FM 21-10 (4-02.10). *Field Hygiene and Sanitation.* MCRP 4-11.1D. 21 June 2000.

FM 90-13. *River Crossing Operations.* MCWP 3-17.1. 26 January 1998.

*FM 101-5-1. *Operational Terms and Graphics.* MCRP 5-2A. 30 September 1997.

TM 8-227-12. *Armed Services Blood Program Joint Blood Program Handbook.* NAVMED P-6530; AFH 44-152. 21 January 1998.

*This source was also used to develop this publication.

Army Publications

AR 220-1. *Unit Status Reporting*. 1 September 1997.
AR 310-25. *Dictionary of United States Army Terms (Short Title: AD)*. 15 October 1983. (Reprinted with basic including Change 1, 21 May 1986.)
FM 100-5. *Operations*. 14 June 1993.
FM 100-7. *Decisive Force: The Army in Theater Operations*. 31 May 1995.
FM 101-5. *Staff Organization and Operations*. 31 May 1997.

DOCUMENTS NEEDED

These documents must be available to the intended users of this publication.

Joint and Multiservice Publications

FM 3-100. *Chemical Operations Principles and Fundamentals*. MCWP 3-3.7.1. 8 May 1996.

Army Publications

AR 30-21. *The Army Field Feeding System*. 24 September 1990.
AR 40-3. *Medical, Dental, and Veterinary Care*. 30 July 1999.
AR 40-5. *Preventive Medicine*. 15 October 1990.
AR 40-35. *Preventive Dentistry*. 26 March 1989.
AR 40-61. *Medical Logistics Policies and Procedures*. 25 January 1995.
AR 40-66. *Medical Record Administrative and Health Care Documentation*. 3 May 1999.
AR 40-216. *Neuropsychiatry and Mental Health*. 10 August 1984.
AR 71-32. *Force Development and Documentation—Consolidated Policies*. 3 March 1997.
AR 700-138. *Army Logistics Readiness and Sustainability*. 16 September 1997.
DA Pam 710-2-1. *Using Unit Supply System (Manual Procedures)*. 31 December 1997.
FM 1-120. *Army Air Traffic Services Contingency and Combat Zone Operations*. 22 May 1995.
FM 3-4. *NBC Protection*. FMFM 11-9. 29 May 1992. (Reprinted with basic including Change1, 28 October 1992; Change 2, 21 February 1996.)
FM 3-5. *NBC Decontamination*. FMFM 11-10. 17 November 1993.
FM 3-50. *Smoke Operations*. 4 December 1990.
FM 4-02.17. *Preventive Medicine Services*. 28 August 2000.
FM 4-02.24 (8-10-24). *Area Support Medical Battalion—Tactics, Techniques, and Procedures*. 28 August 2000.
*FM 8-10 (4-02). *Health Service Support in a Theater of Operations*. 1 March 1991.
*FM 8-10-1 (4-02.6). *The Medical Company—Tactics, Techniques, and Procedures*. 29 December 1994.
*FM 8-10-3 (4-02.3). *Division Medical Operations Center—Tactics, Techniques, and Procedures*. 12 November 1996.

*FM 8-10-4 (4-02.4). *Medical Platoon Leaders' Handbook—Tactics, Techniques, and Procedures.* 16 November 1990.

*FM 8-10-5 (4-02.5). *Brigade and Division Surgeons' Handbook—Tactics, Techniques, and Procedures.* 10 June 1991.

*FM 8-10-6 (4-02.2). *Medical Evacuation in a Theater of Operations—Tactics, Techniques, and Procedures.* 14 April 2000.

FM 8-10-7 (4-02.7). *Health Service Support in a Nuclear, Biological, and Chemical Environment.* 22 April 1993. (Change 1, 26 November 1996.)

*FM 8-10-8 (4-02.8). *Medical Intelligence in a Theater of Operations.* 7 July 1989.

FM 8-10-9 (4-02.9). *Combat Health Logistics in a Theater of Operations—Tactics, Techniques, and Procedures.* 3 October 1995.

FM 8-10-18 (4-02.18). *Veterinary Service—Tactics, Techniques, and Procedures.* 22 August 1997.

FM 8-10-19 (4-02.19). *Dental Service Support in a Theater of Operations.* 12 May 1993.

*FM 8-42 (4-02.42). *Combat Health Support in Stability Operations and Support Operations.* 27 October 1997.

*FM 8-51 (4-02.51). *Combat Stress Control in a Theater of Operations—Tactics, Techniques, and Procedures.* 29 September 1994. (Change 1, 30 January 1998.)

*FM 8-55 (4-02.55). *Planning for Health Service Support.* 9 September 1994.

FM 8-230 (4-02.230). *Medical Specialist.* 24 August 1984.

FM 9-43-1. *Maintenance Operations and Procedures.* 21 February 1997.

FM 11-43. *The Signal Leaders' Guide.* 12 June 1995.

FM 11-55. *Mobile Subscriber Equipment (MSE) Operations.* 22 June 1999.

FM 17-95. *Cavalry Operations.* 24 December 1996.

FM 20-3. *Camouflage, Concealment and Decoys.* 30 August 1999.

*FM 21-10-1 (4-25.12). *Unit Field Sanitation Team.* 11 October 1989.

FM 22-51 (4-02.22). *Leaders' Manual for Combat Stress Control.* 29 September 1994.

*FM 24-1. *Signal Support in the AirLand Battle.* 15 October 1990.

FM 24-24. *Signal Data References: Signal Equipment.* 29 December 1994.

*FM 27-10. *The Law of Land Warfare.* 18 July 1956. (Reprinted with basic including Change 1, 15 July 1976.)

FM 34-54. *Technical Intelligence.* 30 January 1998.

*FM 63-2. *Division Support Command, Armored, Infantry, and Mechanized Infantry Divisions.* 20 May 1991.

*FM 63-2-1. *Division Support Command, Light Infantry, Airborne, and Air Assault Divisions.* 16 November 1992. (Reprinted with basic including Change 1, 20 September 1994.)

FM 63-2-2. *Division Support Command (Digitized).* To be printed.

*FM 63-20. *Forward Support Battalion.* 26 February 1990.

*FM 63-21. *Main Support Battalion.* 7 August 1990.

FM 63-20-1. *Forward Support Battalion (Digitized).* To be printed.

FM 63-21-1. *Division Support Battalion (Digitized).* To be printed.

FM 63-23-2. *Division Aviation Support Battalion (Digitized).* To be printed.

*FM 100-10. *Combat Service Support.* 3 October 1995.

FM 100-17. *Mobilization, Development, Redeployment, Demobilization.* 28 October 1992.

FM 101-5. *Staff Organization and Operations.* 31 May 1997.

SB 8-75 S1. *Department of the Army Supply Bulletin Army Medical Supply Information.* 20 January 2000. (Expires 1 year from date of issue.)

TB 38-750-2. *Maintenance Management Procedures for Medical Equipment.* 12 April 1987. (Reprinted with basic including Changes 1—3, 1 November 1989.)

Department of the Army Forms

DA Form 2404. *Equipment Inspection and Maintenance Worksheet.* 1 April 1979.
DA Form 8007-R. *Individual Medical History (LRA).* November 1996.

Department of Defense Forms

DD Form 314. *Preventive Maintenance Schedule and Record.* 1 December 1953.
DD Form 1380. *US Field Medical Card.* December 1991.
DD Form 2163. *Medical Equipment Verification/Certification.* 1 November 1978.
DD Form 2164. *X-ray Verification/Certification Worksheet.* 1 November 1978.

READINGS RECOMMENDED

These readings contain relevant supplemental information.

Joint and Multiservice Publications

AR 190-8. *Enemy Prisoners of War, Retained Personnel, Civilian Internees, and other Detainees.* OPNAVINST 3461.6; AFJI 31-304; MCO 3461.1. 1 October 1997.
FM 8-9. *NATO Handbook on the Medical Aspects of NBC Defensive Operations AMEDP-6 (B), Part I—Nuclear, Part II—Biological, Part III-Chemical.* NAVMED P-5059; AFJMAN 44-151V1V2V3). 1 February 1996.

Army Publications

FM 5-424. *Theater of Operations Electrical Systems.* 25 June 1997.
FM 12-6. *Personnel Doctrine.* 9 September 1994.
FM 19-1. *Military Police Support for the AirLand Battle.* 23 May 1988.
FM 19-4. *Military Police Battlefield Circulation Control, Area Security, and Enemy Prisoners of War Operations.* 7 May 1993.
FM 19-40. *Enemy Prisoners of War, Civilian Internees, and Detained Persons.* 27 February 1976.
FM 34-3. *Intelligence Analysis.* 15 March 1990.
FM 41-10. *Civil Affairs Operations.* 14 Febuary 2000.
FM 57-38. *Pathfinder Operations.* 9 April 1993.
FM 63-3. *Corps Support Command.* 30 September 1993.
FM 71-3. *The Armored and Mechanized Infantry Brigade.* 8 January 1996.
FM 71-100. *Division Operations.* 28 August 1996.
FM 100-103. *Army Airspace Command and Control in a Combat Zone.* 7 October 1987.

INDEX

References are to paragraph numbers except where specified otherwise.

By Order of the Secretary of the Army:

ERIC K. SHINSEKI
General, United States Army
Chief of Staff

Official:

Administrative Assistant to the
Secretary of the Army
0029301

DISTRIBUTION:

Active Army, Army National Guard, and U.S. Army Reserve: To be distributed in accordance with the initial distribution number 115831, requirements for FM 4-02.21.